MW00810761

TAKE *Your* SEAT

Cover design by: Jason Long for J.L. Designs Creative Group
Cover photo by: Blake Martin Productions, Voodoo Photography

ISBN: 978-1-959095-58-3   1 2 3 4 5 6 7 8 9 10

Printed in the United States of America

TAKE *Your* SEAT

DR. JERMONE T. GLENN

AVAIL

First, I want to dedicate this book to my family.
Thank you for all the sacrifices you made for me and
with me on this journey. You risked a lot to follow me.
I honor my wife Erica, my son Josiah, my daughter
Monae´, and my son Jonathan who never left my
side, even when trusting God got harder and the
leaps of faith He asked us to make became longer.

Second, I'd like to dedicate this book to John Hill, one
co-founder of New Life Church South East in Chicago,
Illinois, who ran all external WOS operations for the orga-
nization. He worked with diligence to establish this mega
ministry and personally guided me on all the inner work-
ings of the organization. He was my sounding board, faith-
fully monitoring my well-being throughout the significant
transition from Senior Pastor to Executive pastor.
From day one, he has modeled the message of Take
Your Seat—*that our lives are delicately intertwined*
with both the large and minute details of God's master
plan. John—your New Life Church family is believing
that God will fully heal you. As you read this dedica-
tion, I hope it reveals how much of an impact you've
had on us and others and that you are loved!

Third, I dedicate this book to all of my teachers, mentors, pastors, and parents for helping on my journey of life. You've helped me live out the story of this book in so many seasons of life. Although I've written a book, Mentors, about you all I can't imagine doing this one without honoring you all. I wouldn't be who I am today if you didn't allow me to sit at your feet and stand on your shoulders.

Finally, I want to dedicate this book to anyone and everyone who has questioned their significance or visibility in their divine purpose. I pray that this book encourages you to delight in helping others accomplish their dreams because when you co-labor with other people to help advance their visions, God will also bring yours to pass. Furthermore, I pray this book encourages each and every reader to consider their seat significant—"spotlight seats" do not necessarily carry more importance. No matter where you are, your position is vital to God's greater plan for His people.

I pray you find power and peace in the seat you're in!

CONTENTS

INTRODUCTION

SHARING MY STORY

This book started as self-therapy. As I journeyed from being a senior pastor and church planter for fourteen years to being an executive pastor, a role I previously held, there were so many lessons learned and questions asked. Very publicly, we transitioned our lives from Grand Rapids, Michigan, to my hometown Chicago, Illinois, to do what was virtually unheard of. We were merging in ministry for greater kingdom impact.

I knew my partner in ministry, John Hannah, well before coming to New Life. Not only were we brothers in ministry, but he was also one of my closest friends. So coming to New Life felt like something I knew well. But New Life needed to get to know me. The tension between new and old is never new, but the constant evolution between two leaders made me realize how challenging it can be to be the second man.

9

There are many dynamic duos in culture for us to draw from, and in every pair, there is the person in command to whom people gravitate and the other leader. Think about it: Kobe and Shaq, Jordan and Pippen, Batman and Robin, L.A. Reid and Babyface, Ben and Jerry, Bugs and Daffy, and countless other duos show us how powerful partnerships can be. Outside looking in, it's simple. Being part of a duo demands you understand that purpose has partners, especially coming from a senior leadership position.

> **Being part of a duo demands you understand that purpose has partners.**

You don't know leadership drama until people try to drive division through comparison, both knowingly and unknowingly. It was a difficult concept for people to understand. Who's doing what? Who is replacing too? Are styles of leading and preaching different? And because we were modeling something that was unfamiliar onlookers didn't know how to accept us together. So naturally, they tried to compare us. But we refused to fall into that trap. There was no competition between us, instead we celebrated each other's uniqueness. People, not so much as first. We can laugh at these things now, but at the time, they took getting used to.

As a senior leader, the weight of a decision is all on you. In this new capacity, as an executive, you are opening yourself up to and inviting all conversations and perspectives around a shared decision. We had to learn together, and people are curious as to how we got it right. Honestly, we're still working on it, we don't always get it right.

First, we are purpose partners. Although John offered me to come in and partner with him, I understood my role and assignment. And it works because we didn't orchestrate it; God did. Because we are in covenant with Him, we are committed to growing together. God gives grace for our unity. This isn't an equal partnership, it's a purposeful partnership and that makes all the difference. It takes leadership capacity on both sides for us to manage well. Thankfully, I have decades of experience being a second man. Still, it was a big change for me.

What I didn't expect was that so many people would be invested and interested in our process. God kept revealing the concept of the second man to me, and the more I explored my life and observed the experiences of those around me, I realized every leader serves another leader at some point in their life. The skills and pressures needed to lead well in that position aren't commonly discussed. The fear of losing yourself in someone else's dream is real. The idea that you could be forgotten stays in the back of your brain. How do you give your all to serving someone else's dream? Do you ever get the chance to fulfill yours? We become so engrossed in ourselves that we forget God calls us to other people.

I realized that the problem wasn't with being the second man—but in understanding how a person leads no matter what seat they're in. Everyone is a leader. Some people lead households, and others lead household brands. Both are necessary, and each is exactly where and how it should be. All seats deserve honor and respect because they have been ordained for us by God for whatever season we are in. The key is not to become apathetic when you feel like you're not the authority. We have to learn to be content in the leadership roles that God gives us.

However, comparison comes in and gnaws away at our desire to lead from an authentic space. Suddenly, we all have to be number one. We all have to be seated in the most prominent place. That's not reality. While we can all lead, we aren't all called to every area all the time. Instead, when we align with God and where He's calling us to lead, incredible things happen. My goal isn't to direct you to where you are supposed to lead. My job is to share insight about how you can lead well from any seat God calls you to.

What seat are you sitting in?
See it; Seize it!

That's when the narrative shifts from the second man to *Take Your Seat*. This is for leaders who desire to align themselves with God's plan to further His kingdom agenda on the earth. It's like Rosa Parks taking her seat on the bus. She had no idea what would spark from that moment, but one act in alignment sparked a movement that brought a revolution to our culture in America. I believe there are precise moments like that for every believer, during which God wants to do something extraordinary in your life that will also benefit many people around you. If you do that by climbing the ladder, great. If you don't, great. What seat are you sitting in? See it; Seize it!

CHAPTER 1

SUBMITTING TO YOUR SEAT

Who are you? Most people answer this question with what they do and the roles they play. We try to categorize pieces of ourselves in relatable ways to our audience. Oftentimes, titles, occupations, experiences, and relationships are things we highlight in our introductions. We live in a world where positional leadership is the primary focus of our culture, and it's easy to feel "less than" if we're not in charge.

But what does that mean for the rest of us? Does that instantly make us less important? Does it mean we don't have a valuable contribution to make? The truth is, it's easy to get caught up in titles and positions, but those things don't define who we are.

Focusing on positional leadership can make you feel inferior if you're not careful. On the surface, it seems more powerful to say you're the chief executive officer than the executive assistant. It's more prestigious to be the presiding judge than the courtroom stenographer. Everyone knows the judge by name and reputation, but we rarely think about the janitor. Having been both the CEO and the janitor, I know this to be true.

The call to leadership is a call to greatness. It is a call to impact the lives of others and to bring about positive change in the world. Oftentimes, though, those who are called to leadership feel overwhelmed, overlooked, and forgotten in their ministry. They feel as though they are just a number in a large organization; they have no real sense of purpose or identity.

I am. THEREFORE, I DO.

This is why it is so important to understand the importance of self-development, self-discovery, and self-love. I am; therefore, I do. When you understand who you are and the unique gifts and talents that God has given you, you can begin to take your seat as a leader in every area of your life. It is only through this process of self-discovery that you can begin to see the true potential to influence God's kingdom that lies within you.

True leadership is about influencing others for good—inspiring and motivating others to reach their full potential. This is the type of leadership that we see demonstrated throughout the kingdom of God, and it is what we are called to embody as leaders.

But the road to leadership is not always easy. Leaders face many challenges and obstacles along the way. They must navigate their own fears and doubts and overcome the negativity and criticism of those around them. Despite these challenges, they must never lose sight of their purpose and calling as leaders.

This book is a solution to feeling overwhelmed, overlooked, and forgotten in ministry. It is a guide to help you know yourself and take your seat as a leader in the kingdom of God. It is a reminder that God never forgets you and that He has a unique plan and purpose for you. Embrace your identity and your calling, and begin leading in every area of your life. This is your moment to make a difference, to impact the lives of others, and to bring about positive change in the world. Take your seat, and lead with confidence, with purpose, and with passion.

I'm going to be honest with you. As you journey through my story of going from a senior pastor at my own church to an executive pastor at a church I didn't plant, you'll see that it has been one of the most challenging experiences of my life. There was something about being the second man that pressed against my identity and forced me to answer the question, *Can I be comfortable sitting where God sets me?* That is the same question I will pose to you: Can *you* be comfortable taking your seat?

Ironically, I've taught this lesson for more than thirteen years in ministry. I have always been about translating power to the pews. I believe *everyone is a leader,* and I've pushed that message in my church for years. Instead of the traditional models of hierarchy, we employ ground leadership on our teams. Everyone focuses on their strengths and executes their tasks well.

At first, it is a struggle for some people to grasp. But as time goes on, we've been able to do more—faster and better than most. We have the power to practice this leadership development system in our organization, and it has helped our members become some of the most productive leaders in every sector across our community. Once they've understood who they are, it hasn't mattered where they went. They've led well.

> **It's not about who you lead.**
> **It's about how you lead.**

I know we are in a culture that teaches us to always be first—to be the leader, the entrepreneur, and the boss. Anything less than that seems less important, but a school won't be a healthy, safe, and thriving environment for children to learn without teachers, support staff, and maintenance. A CEO without a team is rendered useless. And a pastor without a leadership team is overworked and without purpose. I am here to challenge you that it's not about who you lead. It's about how you lead. You are the first leader of your life, and that doesn't change no matter where you are seated.

This is easy to say but harder to wrap your mind around. It took me a while to get here too. God has used my life—time and time again—to prove this point to me. If I am me wherever I go, then I am leading from the seat He gave me. However, before people can get to that point, they have to learn to see seats for what they are—temporary places to reign and rest as God leads.

In this book, we will discover how leaders serving other leaders can be comfortable in their identity and extend pieces of themselves into other people's experiences and make them better.

SEE YOUR SEAT

When you're a leader serving other leaders, you become seated in their vision, and the only way you can do that is to understand the vision you have for your life. That's how you identify when a seat is a good fit for you. It's called alignment. If there isn't synergy between your vision and the vision you serve, you may be in the right seat but at the wrong table.

When my wife and I were getting serious about our relationship, there was a moment she realized that this would be the final and most significant romantic relationship of her life. She saw my vision and my life plans all laid out, and she could see herself in them. The vision I had for my life harmonized with the vision she had for hers. Our skills complemented each other. Our aspirations were bigger than either of us, but by working together, we could accomplish both. And my wife was never concerned that her dreams would take a back seat to mine because she could see the concept of a dream within a dream. Her dream could still be realized in the context of mine, so we were in alignment.

We can't afford to jump into working relationships without the same diligence. It doesn't matter if the salary, title, and role are perfect if the alignment isn't there. You have to stop and think about what you want to do, where you want to do it, and how it aligns with the dreams you carry in your heart.

As a child, we all have great dreams of what we want to become in life. We imagine ourselves as astronauts, actors, or even superheroes. However, as we grow older, reality sets in, and we find ourselves on a different path than the one we originally envisioned. Dr. Myles Munroe, one of my mentors, once said, "The greatest tragedy in life is not death, but a life without purpose."[1] It's important to have a purpose and a dream that drives us forward. Our dreams give us direction, motivation, and a sense of fulfillment.

When I was a teenager, I knew that I was going to impact youth. I was going to be in media and entertainment. I was in a group called Klockwork. We were one demo tape away from heading out on our sold-out worldwide tour. That was my dream. That's not what I am doing today.

> **Just because we're not living the exact dream we had as children doesn't mean we're not in alignment with the ideologies of our youth.**

1   Dr. Myles Munroe, *In Pursuit of Purpose* (Shippensburg, PA: Destiny Image, 2015).

But here's the thing. Just because we're not living the exact dream we had as children doesn't mean we're not in alignment with the ideologies of our youth. We may not have become the astronauts we dreamed of being as children, but we might be working in the field of science or technology which is still a step closer to our childhood dream. We may not have become movie stars, but we might be working in the film industry. It's funny how life works out sometimes.

If we trace back to the common themes of our lives, we might find that we *are* living the dream we've always had for ourselves. Our passions, interests, and values may have evolved, but they are still driving forces in our lives. Our experiences and education may have shaped us differently, but they are still contributing to our personal and professional growth.

It's important to recognize that the journey to one's dream is not always a straight line. We encounter obstacles and setbacks. These are not roadblocks; rather, they're detours that can lead us to our ultimate destination. Sometimes we have to reflect on the path of our lives to understand exactly where we're supposed to be. Long before you take your seat, you have to envision it—see it for what it's meant to be: a throne from which you lead your life.

The journey to your dream is not always a straight line.

The key is for us to have a clear vision of what we want to achieve and a strong desire to pursue it. Ultimately, our dreams should not be limited to just ourselves. I always say that if your dreams only include you, then they aren't big enough. We should strive to make a positive impact on the world and make a difference in the lives of those around us. That's what makes us leaders.

You may be thinking that everyone has dreams, but there's no way that everyone on earth is called to serve as the head of something. That's where you're wrong. I've always believed that everyone is a leader. It's just not about who you lead but what you lead and how. Positional leadership is only one form and the lowest form at that.

Today, many leaders have traded their authority because their dreams had the audacity to turn out differently than they imagined. Instead of taking their seats, they are playing musical chairs in hopes that one day, it will be their turn to finally sit in the coveted number one seat. Chasing after it, they never realize the dream that they had for their lives was within reach.

The truth is you're more powerful sitting in your seat than you will ever be playing musical chairs for someone else's. The concept in itself is against the way we operate in the kingdom of God. When you compete for something that's not yours, you never really win.

Sometimes, the line is blurred between your original dream and what culture has caused you to desire. That's why I challenge people to evaluate their past to elevate their future. You were called to live out an idea and purpose before you were born. This means that although you've developed and matured along the way, you've always had the same reasons for existing. Without the limitations of imagination and the responsibilities of adulthood, we can embrace our dreams with awe in our youth.

Evaluate your past to elevate your future.

What if those dreams aren't as straightforward as we anticipated? When we hit a roadblock, it's easy to become discouraged and lose sight of our vision. We may even question if we're on the right path. But the truth is that progress is not always a straight line. It's often a zigzag, with detours and unexpected turns.

It's important to understand that just because the path may look different than we imagined, it doesn't mean we should give up on our vision. Sometimes, it's the unexpected turn that leads us to our destination. We must keep moving forward, even if it's not in the direction we initially planned. We must trust that every step we take is bringing us closer to our vision, even if we can't see it yet.

In fact, it's often the setbacks and obstacles that refine our vision and make it stronger. It's during these times that we discover what we're truly made of, what we're willing to fight for, and what we truly believe in. The challenges we face bring clarity to our vision and help us focus on what's truly important.

One example of this is the story of Thomas Edison. He tried over ten thousand times to invent the light bulb before he finally succeeded. When asked about his failures, he famously said, "I have not failed 10,000 times—I've successfully found 10,000 ways that will not work."[2] His vision of creating a practical electric light was progressive, and each failed attempt brought him closer to his goal.

The Bible talks about a young man named Joseph in the book of Genesis. He lived thousands of years ago, yet his story still resonates with people today. He was the son of Jacob, one of the patriarchs of the Old Testament. Joseph was his father's favorite son, and this favoritism caused resentment among his brothers. To make matters worse, Joseph had a series of vivid dreams which indicated that he would one day rule over his family. This only added to his brothers' jealousy and contempt for him.

One day, Jacob sent Joseph to check on his brothers, who were tending to their family's flocks. When his brothers saw Joseph coming, they decided to kill him. However, his brother Reuben convinced the others to throw Joseph into a pit instead. When a caravan of traders passed by, the brothers sold Joseph to them for twenty pieces of silver.

Joseph was taken to Egypt and sold to Potiphar, an officer of Pharaoh. Joseph served Potiphar well and was eventually put in charge of his household. However, Potiphar's wife falsely accused Joseph of trying to seduce her, and he was thrown into prison.

Even in prison, Joseph continued to use his gifts and talents to serve others. He interpreted dreams for his fellow prisoners, including

---

2 Erica R. Hendry, "7 Epic Fails Brought to You By the Genius Mind of Thomas Edison, *Smithsonian Magazine*, 20 Nov. 2013, https://www.smithsonianmag.com/innovation/7-epic-fails-brought-to-you-by-the-genius-mind-of-thomas-edison-180947786/.

DR. JERMONE T. GLENN

Pharaoh's chief cupbearer and the chief baker. When Pharaoh himself had a series of troubling dreams, the chief cupbearer remembered Joseph and recommended him to the king.

Joseph was brought before Pharaoh and interpreted his dreams. They indicated that Egypt would experience seven years of plenty followed by seven years of famine. Pharaoh was so impressed with Joseph's wisdom that he put him in charge of the entire nation, second only to Pharaoh himself.

Under Joseph's leadership, Egypt stored up enough grain during the seven years of plenty to sustain the nation during the seven years of famine. Joseph's brothers, who were suffering from famine in their own land, came to Egypt to buy grain. They did not recognize Joseph, who had become a powerful and wealthy ruler in the land of Egypt.

Joseph tested his brothers and ultimately revealed his true identity to them. He forgave them for their betrayal and provided for their needs during the famine. He even invited his father, Jacob, and the rest of the family to live in Egypt and provided for their needs as well.

Joseph's story is a powerful example of God's faithfulness and providence to bring a dream to pass. Despite the jealousy and hatred of his brothers, the false accusations of Potiphar's wife, and years spent in prison, God used Joseph's gifts and talents to bring about His divine plan. Joseph's story reminds us that even when our dreams are seemingly shattered, and we face insurmountable obstacles, God is still at work in our lives. He is faithful to His promises and will use even the most difficult circumstances for our good and His glory.

> **We can lead authentically
> in every space.**

I often ask myself if Joseph ever looked back and saw the way God brought his dream about. Was he reflective about his journey or so immersed in it that he couldn't see it all unfold? Thankfully, we get to use this story as the basis for how we can lead authentically in every space, serve other leaders, and still live out our original God-given dreams.

HOW DO YOU IDENTIFY A GOD DREAM?

Not all dreams are from God. Some ideas we carry come from the culture of our homes and communities. I've learned that it's essential that we don't let these experiences evict God's vision from our minds. Other times, we become so consumed with a piece of a dream that we don't take a step back to see the big picture. We must be discerning and test every dream against God's Word.

So how do we know if a dream is from God? First, we must ask ourselves if the dream aligns with God's character and His Word. Our God is a God of truth, love, and justice. If a dream goes against these principles, it is likely not from God.

Second, we must ask ourselves if the dream leads us closer to God. Our God desires an intimate relationship with us, and He will use our dreams to draw us closer to Him. If a dream encourages us to pursue God more passionately, it may be from Him.

Third, we must ask ourselves if the dream produces good fruit. Our God is a God of goodness and mercy, and He desires that we bear good fruit in our lives. If a dream leads to positive outcomes, it may be from God.

Fourth, we must ask ourselves if the dream persists. Sometimes, God will give us a dream that stays with us over time rather than just being a passing thought. If a dream continues to stick with us, it may be from God.

Finally, we must ask ourselves if the dream brings peace. Our God is a God of peace, and He desires that we have peace in our hearts. If a dream brings a sense of peace and clarity, it may be from God.

Discerning the voice of God is not just about our dreams. It's about listening to His voice in every area of our lives. We must be willing to follow His leading, even when it goes against our own desires.

John Maxwell, a great leader and man of God, wrote about the importance of listening to God's voice in his book *The 21 Irrefutable Laws of Leadership*.[3] He teaches us that we can hear God's voice through prayer, Scripture, wise counsel, and the Holy Spirit's leading. And we must be open and willing to act on His guidance.

---

3   John C. Maxwell, *The 21 Irrefutable Laws of Leadership* (Nashville, TN: Thomas Nelson, 2007).

> **The closer you get to God, the simpler it becomes to identify His thoughts, dreams, and plans.**

I believe the closer you get to God, the simpler it becomes to identify His thoughts, dreams, and plans for us, not that we won't ever have moments when we question. We just know what to do with those questions when they arise. I frequently conduct three checks on my dreams:

1. Expansive—It's bigger than me.
2. Encompassing—It aligns with God's plans for me.
3. Everlasting—It never goes away.

We can see this blueprint in the dreams Joseph had when we are first introduced to him. As we journey through Joseph's story, we'll see how his life can inspire and guide us in our own lives. We'll learn how to navigate through difficult circumstances and remain true to who we are. We'll discover how to trust in God's plan for our lives, even when it doesn't make sense. Joseph's story shows us that if we lean into our God dreams, no matter where at the table we are sitting, we will be in a position of power. Imagine your influence in the kingdom if you'll open your heart and mind to the lessons that Joseph's life has to offer and allow them to transform you from the inside out. What's stopping you?

CHAPTER 2

SEEING YOUR VISION
GENESIS 37:1-11

When we start to look at our dreams, we can't forget to look at the dreams of those who have gone before us. Taking your seat and embracing where you are at the table can't happen without first embracing yourself. When you explore your history, you embark on a journey with clarity and consciousness about God's desires for you. I know that's a lot of work when you simply want to learn how to impact change within your sphere of influence, but leadership has to be personal to be purposeful.

> **Leadership has to be personal to be purposeful.**

Those close to me often tease me about how reflective I am as a person. But that gives me understanding, and understanding gives me the power to lead my life well. I understand the conditions that I was born in and for. I asked my parents when and how I was conceived because that's important to my temperament. I understand my birthday is Earth Day, but it was also Resurrection Sunday. I am aware of every person who has poured into my life. These pieces help me see the vision God has for me because they complete my puzzle.

> **From the pit to the palace, Joseph's life is a picture of God working everything together for our good.**

Perhaps that's why I love the story of Joseph so much. From the pit to the palace, his life is a picture of everything working together for good. In order to understand him a bit better, let's do a quick Bible study of his lineage.

Joseph was the son of Jacob, who was later named Israel, and Rachel. The story of Jacob and Rachel is a beautiful and complex love story woven throughout the pages of the Bible. Their relationship was full of twists and turns. It was marked by deceit, heartbreak, and deep love.

At the beginning of their story in Genesis 29, Jacob was on the run from his brother Esau. Esau and Jacob were twins, but Esau had been born first, so the family position and the wealth that came with it should have passed to him. However, through a series of manipulations, Jacob deceived both Esau and their father into bestowing the birthright on Jacob instead. Fearing for her son's life, Rebekah sent Jacob—who had always been her favorite—to the land of her people where he would be safe.

We next see Jacob at a well on his uncle's land. It was here that he glimpsed his cousin Rachel and fell in love with her at first sight. Immediately drawn to her, Jacob agreed to work for her father, Laban, for seven years in order to marry her. This demonstrates the power of love and the willingness to work hard for the things we desire in life.

However, Laban deceived Jacob by giving him Leah to marry instead of Rachel. Leah was Rachel's older sister. Genesis 29:17 (ESV, emphasis mine) says that "*Leah's eyes were weak*, but Rachel was beautiful in form and appearance." You can imagine how disappointed he was to find out he had done all that work—and dreamt of beautiful Rachel all those years—only to get Leah instead. We know that life is not always fair, and sometimes, we must persevere through difficult and unjust circumstances. Jacob did not give up on his love for Rachel, and he agreed to work another seven years as well in order to marry her.

Jacob's love for Rachel is evident throughout their story. Many times, the Bible describes that Jacob favored Rachel over Leah. And he loved Rachel's children—when she finally had them—over Leah's and worked hard to provide for his family. This shows us the importance of loving deeply and putting in the effort to make our relationships work.

Rachel, though, struggled with infertility and felt intense jealousy toward her sister who was able to have many children. This reminds us that we all have struggles and challenges in life, but we must persevere and trust in God's plan for our lives.

Rachel eventually conceived and gave birth to a son, whom she named Joseph, because she said, "The Lord shall add to me another son" (Genesis 30:24, KJV). Despite how difficult it had been for Rachel to conceive in the first place, she obviously believed that God would add more children to her family. This is a reminder that even in the midst of our struggles, we must have faith and trust in God's provision and blessings.

So by the time we encounter Joseph in Genesis 37, there's a lot of context to grasp. He is Jacob's favorite son, presumably because of all that happened before him. He is a seed from his birth. His mother named him Joseph meaning "He will add," and declared God would give them *another* son. That's why he had to be "pitted," but we will get to that later. Joseph's birth was seen as a special blessing because Rachel had been barren those many years before conceiving him.

Joseph's childhood was likely a mix of privilege and difficulty. As the son of Jacob's favorite wife, he was likely given more attention and resources than his brothers. However, this favoritism also made him a target of his siblings' jealousy and resentment, enough so that they saw him as a threat to their position in the family—a nuisance to be eliminated. Joseph's earlier life was also marked by tragedy and upheaval. Rachel died giving birth to his brother Benjamin, his father's favoritism caused tension and division in the family, and Joseph's immaturity got the better of him sometimes.

JOSEPH'S DREAM

This is the account of Joseph's early life:

> *Joseph, a young man of seventeen, was tending the flocks with his brothers, the sons of Bilhah and the sons of Zilpah, his father's wives, and he brought their father a bad report about them.*
>
> *Now Israel loved Joseph more than any of his other sons because he had been born to him in his old age; and [Jacob] made an ornate robe for [Joseph]. When his brothers saw that their father loved him more than any of them, they hated him and could not speak a kind word to him.*
>
> *Joseph had a dream, and when he told it to his brothers, they hated him all the more. He said to them, "Listen to this dream I had: We were binding sheaves of grain out in the field when suddenly my sheaf rose and stood upright, while your sheaves gathered around mine and bowed down to it."*
>
> *His brothers said to him, "Do you intend to reign over us? Will you actually rule us?" And they hated him all the more because of his dream and what he had said.*
>
> *Then he had another dream, and he told it to his brothers. "Listen," he said, "I had another dream, and this time the sun and moon and eleven stars were bowing down to me."*
>
> *When he told his father as well as his brothers, his father rebuked him and said, "What is this dream you had? Will your*

*mother and I and your brothers actually come and bow down to
the ground before you?" His brothers were jealous of him, but his
father kept the matter in mind. —Genesis 37:2-11*

YOUR DREAM

What happens when God shows you a vision? Where and with
whom do you share that vision? Who sits in the seat of the dream
interpreter in your life?

> **We don't need vision vultures
> to pick apart our ideas.**

Have you ever had a really good idea, but you told it to the wrong
person? Before the words rolled off your lips, that person shredded
the dream into a million pieces, leaving you feeling empty, violated,
and upset! We don't need vision vultures to pick apart our ideas. We
need incubators who can interpret and incubate our ideas, so they can
grow. Of course, when it's time to execute them, we need discerning
individuals to poke holes in our dreams, so they can be tested, and
we won't fail. But not when you are simply sharing.

Joseph's family was definitely made up of vision vultures. He
went to them, sharing the dreams he had. Instead of understanding,
they dismantled what he told them. They couldn't see past Joseph's

promotion or protect his discovery. As the adage goes, people often fear what they don't understand.

In Joseph's dream, everyone had a role to play. The brothers couldn't comprehend that they were stars. How powerful to be in the stratosphere! However, because their shine wasn't the brightest, they tried to diminish Joseph's. While he was looking for someone to interpret the dream, they interrupted it.

Vision is validated in identity. It's clear from the text later in the story that these boys didn't know who they were. They knew what their mothers called them out of their pain, but fathers give language to one's life. Israel, their father, hadn't done that yet, according to the text.

While things may have gone differently for Joseph had his family accepted his dream, we can't say what that would look like. What we can deduce is that God needs to seal a vision in you so that it is secure before you share it.

As leaders who serve leaders, we are often misunderstood. But that's okay. Everyone isn't meant to see the same thing. Perspective helps us solve problems faster. God grants each of us a unique opportunity to see through our gifts, heritage, and history. In that way, we are similar to Joseph.

It's pertinent to your success to understand your vision. But perhaps more importantly, your ability to see other people's vision properly makes you incredibly valuable. A lesson we can all carry with us as we serve is to not become bitter as the brothers did. You will be called to interpret the dreams of many because you are trusted and gifted as a second-in-command. You have to learn to do it without complaint. As we will discover later in the story, this was a key to Joseph's growth and popularity in his future.

> **Contentment in your role comes from giving your gift freely.**

Contentment in your role comes from giving your gift freely. If you learn to respond when someone shares their ideas with you, you will gain favor with them. Think of it in reverse. To whom do you go to share your great ideas? For me, that person is my wife. I know she's going to celebrate with me; she's going to help me develop a strategy for execution. She is seated in that position in my life. If she is not secure about being second in that moment, she can ruin the dream for me. And vice versa. When she's the dreamer, I can't be focused on what it means for me. Instead, I ask how I can fit into her dreams to make them a reality.

You want to know what I believe the number one blockage to being able to receive somebody else's dream is? Frustration. When we become frustrated with our own thoughts, dreams, visions, and ideas not coming to pass, we project that onto other people. That's why we have to be in tune with the God of our dreams first. If we can't pursue our dreams, we can become discouraged and distracted trying to help somebody else pursue theirs.

This can cause a person to forfeit their seat. I want to help you eliminate it before this idea is demonstrated in your life. To do so, we must take a moment to eliminate all outside distractions. I want you to put your titles on hold, set your rules aside, and take a moment to focus on the reason God created you.

> **Having a personal dream qualifies you to handle somebody else's.**

Having a personal dream qualifies you to handle somebody else's dream. It is the breeding ground for you to understand how to bring theirs to life. If you know how you want your ideas handled, it better qualifies you to handle somebody else's. Most of us are walking around blind when it comes to our own dreams. We believe that if our dreams don't look exactly as they did in our minds, then we have failed to achieve them. We become fearful of failure, so we forget our ability to achieve.

Let's walk through an exercise to help you gain a better understanding of your dreams and how your talents, gifts, and abilities work together. The process of understanding your dream can be a deeply reflective and rewarding experience. I've outlined a guide to help you figure it out.

1. What activities make you feel the most alive and fulfilled? Research by psychologist Mihaly Csikszentmihalyi has shown

that people experience a state of flow when they are engaged in activities that challenge them but also match their skills.[4] These activities often provide a sense of purpose and enjoyment. Reflect on the activities that make you feel the most engaged and energized, and consider how you can incorporate them into your life purpose.

2. What are your core values and beliefs? Our values and beliefs can guide us in discovering our life purpose. Consider what matters most to you and how you want to contribute to the world. For example, if you value social justice, your life purpose might involve working toward greater equality or advocating for marginalized groups.

3. What are the common themes in your life experiences? Reflect on the experiences in your life that have brought you the most joy, fulfillment, and growth. What common themes do you notice? For example, if you've always enjoyed teaching, your life purpose might involve sharing your knowledge and skills with others.

4. What would you do if money were not a factor? When pursuing their life purpose, many people feel limited by financial considerations. However, imagining a scenario where money is not a factor can help you clarify what truly matters to you. What would you do if you had unlimited resources and could

---

4   Mike Oppland, "8 Traits of Flow According to Mihaly Csikszentmihalyi," *PositivePsychology.com*, 9 Mar. 2023, https://positivepsychology.com/mihaly-csikszentmihalyi-father-of-flow/.

DR. JERMONE T. GLENN

pursue any path you wanted? This exercise can help you uncover your deepest passions and aspirations.

5. How can you contribute to the world in a unique way? Finally, consider what unique gifts and talents you possess that can contribute to the world in a meaningful way. What makes you stand out from others? What do you offer that no one else can? Use these qualities to guide you in discovering your life purpose.

By reflecting on these questions and exploring your own experiences, values, and aspirations, you can begin to identify your life purpose or dream. Keep in mind that discovering your purpose is a lifelong journey, and it's okay to re-vision your vision while in pursuit of purpose. Vision is not permanent, it's progressive. I always say that vision is progressive, meaning it changes as you go. I'm sure Joseph's understanding of his dreams changed along the way too.

> **It's okay to re-vision your vision while in pursuit of purpose. Vision is not permanent, it's progressive.**

Now that you have taken a look at your dreams, what do you think? Are there surprising things that you didn't know were there before? Are you actually living out ideas that you've had from childhood in your life today? I am. Earlier, I told you that I dreamed of impacting youth through media, messaging, and music. At a young age, I associated that with being an R&B superstar. As an adult, I see what God was giving me a glimpse of in my earlier years.

Today, I lead tens of thousands of people, including younger generations, to know God better. I further Christian culture through media, messaging, and music. It's as a pastor. Who would have expected that? I didn't. But once I learned to reconcile the differences, I knew what seats I'd been called to sit in. I sit in them even now. I can handle a seat as second-in-command because I see how it allows me not only to serve my dream but also the dreams of others.

What differences do you need to reconcile, so you can serve your dream as well as the dreams of others?

CHAPTER 3

SURVIVING YOUR SEND-OFF

GENESIS 37:12-35

I t's easy to comprehend with your logic that your dreams may look different than you expected, but the experience of it can do damage to your soul. What happens when the marriage you thought would last for a lifetime ends in divorce? Imagine moving and getting denied an apartment—when God promised you a home. It more than stings; it devastates and penetrates to your core.

I've been in ministry for over thirty years. As I write this book, I am not yet fifty years of age. That's how young I was when I accepted the call to lead others! I started ministry as a youth pastor. There wasn't an executive pastor on our staff, so I was very close to the senior pastor.

In fact, he became one of my most influential mentors. The favor that I found with Bishop Rory Marshall was, indeed, uncommon.

It reminds me of the way that Israel, another name for Jacob, showered favor on Joseph. Even though there were other staff members with longer tenure and deeper roots in ministry, and they had been in leadership positions since before I was born, Bishop saw something in me worth cultivating. From that moment, I knew that leadership in ministry was part of my identity.

In a way, you could say that my first job in ministry was as an executive pastor. I fulfilled the functions of a second-in-command. It's how I started the journey, and I was content there. But one day, Bishop Marshall got the call to move from Grand Rapids back to my hometown of Chicago. He spoke to the church in Grand Rapids and told them that God had revealed I was to be their senior pastor. Can you imagine the scoffs of senior and executive team members who were looking at me, a boy in their eyes, in disbelief? There was no way that they were going to accept me as their pastor. The board rejected the proposal emphatically.

Sound familiar? If God was showing me that I was to lead, and He was showing Pastor Marshall, then what was happening? As soon as it was settled that I would not be the senior pastor of the Grand Rapids church, I decided that it was time for me to go too. I moved to Chicago where I would be able to attend college, stay in ministry with Bishop Marshall, and continue to lead the youth—who were now young adults—in ministry.

Not long after I moved, Bishop Marshall was removed from the church. That happened prior to even having his first service. That dream was gone. Then, as time went on and I continued pursuing my assignment to lead, different twists and turns happened.

I met a woman, fell in love, got married, and started a family. After completing my education, I took the opportunity to go through church planting certification. It seemed that my dream of establishing a church, bringing Christ into the culture, leading the youth, and operating as a senior pastor in ministry was coming to pass. I pursued what I believed God was showing me. However, my life was about to undergo one of the most significant changes I'd ever experienced up to this point. My wife realized that she could not take her seat in the dream that I had, and she loved me too much to get in the way of what God was calling me to do. Ultimately, that meant she wanted to get a divorce. How did this happen? How was I pursuing God yet finding myself on the bitter end of what I thought was the most purposeful relationship that I would ever have?

> **I can't be the only one who has ever questioned God.**

I can't be the only one who has ever questioned God. Have you gotten to a point where you didn't understand how what He had said and what you saw aligned, but you'd followed all His directions? If it wasn't one thing, it was another. I could handle the rejection from my church back home. I learned to process through Bishop Marshall's being fired from the church in Chicago. I could still operate in my calling in a new space and place. But how could my dream lead me to the place where my family was being torn apart at the seams?

Joseph dealt with something similar. As he received more favor from his father and had more dreams, the more his brothers began to hate him, and one day, his father sent him off to do something that should have gone smoothly, but it didn't. Instead, Joseph found himself at rock bottom—literally.

THROWN INTO THE PIT

Genesis 37:12-35 takes us to the next part of Joseph's story:

> *Now his brothers had gone to graze their father's flocks near Shechem, and Israel said to Joseph, "As you know, your brothers are grazing the flocks near Shechem. Come, I am going to send you to them."*
>
> *"Very well," he replied.*
>
> *So he said to him, "Go and see if all is well with your brothers and with the flocks, and bring word back to me." Then he sent him off from the Valley of Hebron.*
>
> *When Joseph arrived at Shechem, a man found him wandering around in the fields and asked him, "What are you looking for?"*
>
> *He replied, "I'm looking for my brothers. Can you tell me where they are grazing their flocks?"*
>
> *"They have moved on from here," the man answered. "I heard them say, 'Let's go to Dothan.'"*

DR. JERMONE T. GLENN

So Joseph went after his brothers and found them near Dothan. But they saw him in the distance, and before he reached them, they plotted to kill him.

"Here comes that dreamer!" they said to each other. "Come now, let's kill him and throw him into one of these cisterns and say that a ferocious animal devoured him. Then we'll see what comes of his dreams."

When Reuben heard this, he tried to rescue him from their hands. "Let's not take his life," he said. "Don't shed any blood. Throw him into this cistern here in the wilderness, but don't lay a hand on him." Reuben said this to rescue him from them and take him back to his father.

So when Joseph came to his brothers, they stripped him of his robe—the ornate robe he was wearing—and they took him and threw him into the cistern. The cistern was empty; there was no water in it.

As they sat down to eat their meal, they looked up and saw a caravan of Ishmaelites coming from Gilead. Their camels were loaded with spices, balm and myrrh, and they were on their way to take them down to Egypt.

Judah said to his brothers, "What will we gain if we kill our brother and cover up his blood? Come, let's sell him to the Ishmaelites and not lay our hands on him; after all, he is our brother, our own flesh and blood." His brothers agreed.

So when the Midianite merchants came by, his brothers pulled Joseph up out of the cistern and sold him for twenty shekels of silver to the Ishmaelites, who took him to Egypt.

When Reuben returned to the cistern and saw that Joseph was not there, he tore his clothes. He went back to his brothers and said, "The boy isn't there! Where can I turn now?"

Then they got Joseph's robe, slaughtered a goat and dipped the robe in the blood. They took the ornate robe back to their father and said, "We found this. Examine it to see whether it is your son's robe."

He recognized it and said, "It is my son's robe! Some ferocious animal has devoured him. Joseph has surely been torn to pieces."

Then Jacob tore his clothes, put on sackcloth and mourned for his son many days. All his sons and daughters came to comfort him, but he refused to be comforted. "No," he said, "I will continue to mourn until I join my son in the grave." So his father wept for him.

Joseph was following the plan his father laid out before him. This should have been something simple to do. "Go check on your brothers." Perhaps his dad sent him because it would show his brothers that Joseph was "one of them." Maybe this journey would earn Joseph the recognition of being a hard worker, like his brothers. Maybe the stench of sweat would eliminate the sweet smell of favoritism.

But his very presence infuriated them. I don't want to know what it's like to have my essence cause people to want to execute me. Some of the responses to your dreams are people trying to kill them. There are words that come to strangle the life out of them.

You thought you were on your way to purpose, only to find yourself at the bottom of a pit.

Joseph went from the pit to the palace.

Today, we focus on the idea that Joseph went from the pit to the palace. To truly grasp this concept, we must first acknowledge that he hit the bottom of the pit. Interestingly enough, what he was thrown in was a cistern: a deep hole and underground water system to irrigate the land. I imagine that it was similar to our sinkholes today. However, there was no water in this cistern. That means nothing broke his fall. Instead, he suffered in the hole while his brothers feasted.

Imagine hours going by as you sit in a hole, and the very people who are supposed to live out your dreams with you are the cause of your suffering. To make it worse, they profited off of his misery. However, selling Joseph into slavery wasn't destroying the dream. It was propelling it.

The Bible doesn't tell us much about Joseph's emotional state. But in our humanity, we can understand going from someone's favorite son to a slave. Demoralizing. The dream fades away. Has your dream faded?

Chances are you know what it's like to fail. You may have even hit rock bottom. The pit is where our hope goes to die. It's like a grave marking the finality of our lives. Most of us have let go of something here.

People say Jacob's sons *pitted* Joseph. I say they *planted* him.

People say Jacob's sons pitted Joseph. I say they planted him.

The process of a seed sprouting is a beautiful metaphor for the journey that Joseph experienced while trapped in a pit. Like a seed planted in soil, Joseph was thrown into a dark and challenging situation. At first, it may have seemed like he was trapped and forgotten, with no hope for growth or progress. However, just as a seed requires darkness and moisture to germinate, Joseph's time in the pit provided the opportunity for him to grow and develop in ways that he may not have been able to otherwise.

A seed that is planted must rely on the nutrients in the soil and the conditions around it to grow. As Joseph embraced his circumstances and trusted in God's plan, he began to grow and develop into the leader that he was destined to become. Eventually, just as a seed sprouts and breaks through the soil to reach for the sunlight, Joseph was able to emerge from the pit and lead.

Like a seed that must be planted in order to grow, Joseph's time in the pit was a necessary part of his journey to fulfilling his purpose. It was a challenging and dark time, but it provided the next step for his path. For those who may feel trapped in a situation or overlooked in their role as second-in-command, Joseph's story serves as a reminder that there is always potential for growth and progress, even in the darkest of circumstances. Trusting in God's plan and embracing your circumstances, like a seed planted in soil, can lead to beautiful growth and transformation.

Maybe, though, if you're too close, you can't see it for yourself. One of my favorite psychological tools to help with this is called a lifeline. It involves creating a timeline that charts significant events, emotions, and milestones in one's life. The purpose of the lifeline activity is to help individuals identify patterns and themes in their life, gain a deeper understanding of themselves, and develop insight into their future goals and aspirations.

I want you to create a lifeline. Grab a blank sheet of paper and follow these simple steps:

1. Draw a line across a piece of paper to create a time line of your dream. Label the beginning of the line with your birthdate and the end with the present day.

2. Reflect on the different stages of your life and identify key moments when you felt aligned with this dream. This could be anything from discovering a passion, achieving a goal, or making a meaningful connection with someone.

3. Use symbols, colors, or words to mark these moments on the timeline. You can also write a brief description or memory associated with each moment.

4. Next, look for patterns or themes among the purposeful moments you've identified. Do you notice any common things

or motivations that have guided your actions over time? Do you see how you could be living in your dream and not yet recognize it because your lifeline is still going?

5. Use this insight to clarify your dreams and progress. You can use this knowledge to get a better understanding of your development and hold fast to the dreams God has given you.

Using this lifeline is a remarkable way to see progress when you feel stagnant. Leading others can be a lonely place. Having a lifeline to look back on helps you ensure that you are functioning in your primary role of leadership, personal leadership.

The problem with being in a pit is a lack of focus. You look around for ways to get out. You look up to see what's happening around you. But the best place to look when you're in a pit is within. If I could tell you anything about my pit season, it is that I didn't focus fast enough.

If you can learn that the isolation of the pit teaches you to hold on to God when you are pushed away from the world, you're winning. In dark spaces, you hone your ability to be the light. When you don't know what's going to happen next, you learn how to create it.

> **In dark spaces, you hone your ability to be the light.**

Transition is always sudden. It is an abrupt yet often divine intervention in your process. The people Joseph went to serve severed ties

DR. JERMONE T. GLENN

with him. The people I ran *toward* in Chicago I wanted to run *away from* after my divorce.

The things that rise up against us the most are usually the things that we are assigned to change. Our dreams are a piece of how we do that. If you can hold on to your vision, dream, and ideas in the midst of a dark season, then you gain immense power for the future. You become qualified to sit in any seat God assigns. We will see that is exactly what came to pass in Joseph's life. How are you seeing it come to pass in yours?

CHAPTER 4

STEWARDING YOUR CHARACTER
GENESIS 39:1-20

People never expect you to get over what they do to you, but if you don't, you may become scared and cautious about new people you encounter. Either way, it doesn't matter. God holds you accountable to lead despite the actions of the people who have negatively impacted you.

When I went through my divorce, I didn't want anything to do with church. I was ashamed and angry. I would run from church and try to find other vices, but God always pulled me back in. I would hide in the back pew and still—somehow—be pulled into the grasp of an intercessor or in the line of sight of another pastor.

I had to get out of the pit fast. That's when I ended up serving as the executive pastor for Bishop William C. Abney. You can read the entire story in my book *Mentors*. But the abbreviated version is Bishop Abney pulled me in and favored me in a season when I felt I had been sold into slavery. I was working in the school system of Chicago, but he pulled me back into ministry. He was a connection point for every facet of my future—including my partner, purpose, and wife, who happened to be his granddaughter.

The pitfalls from my past slowly began to fade away. I found safety in this season of my life. Favor and success definitely followed me from Chicago back to Grand Rapids. I was home again. I was leading again. I was serving one of the greatest ministry leaders in the world. It was proof that God trusted me.

> **God will protect and promote you despite the problems you face.**

One of the things we overlook during adversity is the power of our response. God will protect and promote you despite the problems that you face. That is a promise you can hold fast to when you are aligned with Him. Once I made the decision to come out of the pit and give God everything I had, things shifted.

I promise you; Colossians 3:23-24 is an underrated leadership life hack:

> *Whatever you do, work at it with all your heart, as working for the Lord, not for human masters, since you know that you will*

> receive an inheritance from the Lord as a reward. It is the Lord
> Christ you are serving.

This is not only what I did but what I have to believe Joseph did as well, and we'll see it in the next part of his story:

> Now Joseph had been taken down to Egypt. Potiphar, an Egyptian who was one of Pharaoh's officials, the captain of the guard, bought him from the Ishmaelites who had taken him there.
>
> The Lord was with Joseph so that he prospered, and he lived in the house of his Egyptian master. When his master saw that the Lord was with him and that the Lord gave him success in everything he did, Joseph found favor in his eyes and became his attendant. Potiphar put him in charge of his household, and he entrusted to his care everything he owned. From the time he put him in charge of his household and of all that he owned, the Lord blessed the household of the Egyptian because of Joseph. The blessing of the Lord was on everything Potiphar had, both in the house and in the field. So Potiphar left everything he had in Joseph's care; with Joseph in charge, he did not concern himself with anything except the food he ate.
>
> Now Joseph was well-built and handsome, and after a while, his master's wife took notice of Joseph and said, "Come to bed with me!"
>
> But he refused. "With me in charge," he told her, "my master does not concern himself with anything in the house; everything he owns he has entrusted to my care. No one is greater in this house than I am. My master has withheld nothing from me except you, because you are his wife. How then could I do

such a wicked thing and sin against God?" And though she spoke to Joseph day after day, he refused to go to bed with her or even be with her.

One day he went into the house to attend to his duties, and none of the household servants was inside. She caught him by his cloak and said, "Come to bed with me!" But he left his cloak in her hand and ran out of the house.

When she saw that he had left his cloak in her hand and had run out of the house, she called her household servants. "Look," she said to them, "this Hebrew has been brought to us to make sport of us! He came in here to sleep with me, but I screamed. When he heard me scream for help, he left his cloak beside me and ran out of the house."

She kept his cloak beside her until his master came home. Then she told him this story: "That Hebrew slave you brought us came to me to make sport of me. But as soon as I screamed for help, he left his cloak beside me and ran out of the house."

When his master heard the story his wife told him, saying, "This is how your slave treated me," he burned with anger. Joseph's master took him and put him in prison, the place where the king's prisoners were confined. —Genesis 39:1-20

The story of Joseph and Potiphar's wife is one of the most well-known and intriguing narratives in the Bible. It is a story of temptation, betrayal, and, ultimately, redemption. At its core, the story is a powerful reminder that even in the midst of adversity and hardship, you can remain faithful to the calling and find the strength to overcome temptation. Remember your private pain usually leads to public promotion.

> **You can remain faithful to the calling and find the strength to overcome temptation. Remember your private pain usually leads to public promotion.**

When we encountered Joseph again, he was a young Hebrew slave who had been sold into bondage by his brothers. Despite his difficult circumstances, Joseph remained faithful to God and worked hard in the household of his new master, Potiphar. In fact, Joseph was so diligent and trustworthy that Potiphar put him in charge of his entire household, including Potiphar's wife, who is described as a beautiful and seductive woman. She set her sights on Joseph and tried to seduce him, but Joseph resisted her advances and declared that he could not sin against God in this way.

At its surface level, the story of Joseph and Potiphar's wife is a simple tale of sexual temptation and the consequences of giving in to it. However, there is much more going on beneath the surface of the text.

First, it is important to note that Potiphar was a high-ranking official in the court of Pharaoh, the ruler of Egypt. As such, he would have been a powerful and influential man with significant resources at his disposal. This would have made him an attractive target for those seeking to gain favor with Pharaoh. Potiphar's wife, in particular, would have been acutely aware of her husband's status and influence and would have seen Joseph as a means to an end. By seducing him, she would not only be satisfying her own desires but also gaining leverage over Potiphar himself.

Furthermore, it is important to understand the cultural context in which this story takes place. In ancient Egypt, women were generally seen as subordinate to men and were often viewed as objects of sexual desire. As such, Potiphar's wife would have been accustomed to using her sexuality as a means of gaining power and influence.

Joseph, on the other hand, was a Hebrew slave, an outsider in a foreign land. As such, he would have been vulnerable to exploitation and abuse, particularly from those in positions of power. However, Joseph's steadfast faith in God gave him the strength to resist temptation and remain faithful to his calling, despite the potential consequences—another pit. Only this time, the setback landed Joseph in prison. He was incarcerated for something he didn't do.

The saying "To whom much is given, much is required" couldn't ring truer. Oftentimes, I imagine those responsibilities as being more burdensome than a bigger test. What's the worst that could have happened? If Joseph had slipped away with Potiphar's wife, who would have known? It's likely she would keep the secret while he served her. But when her fetishism and infatuation were gone, what would happen? He would become a slave again. Her personal sex slave.

STEWARDING CHARACTER

As a second-in-command leader, you are in one of the most trust-worthy positions you can be in. You, like Joseph, have access to everything. I know this from personal experience. I have had secondary leaders in my life and around my wife when I've been gone. First, I know that I can trust her. I put the most trust in those I grant access to my life.

The more leadership you acquire, the more authority to delegate you have. You may have a driver, a nanny, or an accountant. You've selected each of those people because you can trust them. Can the leaders who put you in place trust you too? This should be a resounding *yes*. If the answer is yes, you are stewarding your character well. If not, you need to review the lessons you learned in the pit.

As a secondary leader, you have the responsibility to steward character well. It's interesting that what's built over time can be ruined overnight. Don't destroy your destiny because of one bad decision. While temptation may come, purpose pulls you to your seat. You can't have a seat if you're secretly trying to sit in someone else's.

> **You can't have a seat if you're secretly trying to sit in someone else's.**

Everything you do in the kingdom of God is a seed. Ultimately, we have to be intentional about how we steward one season because we will reap the harvest of it in another. Had Joseph treated Poti-phar with the anger his brothers deserved, then he would have had to face the consequences. However, because he was upright before God, favor was his.

I believe that leadership skills alone aren't enough when you are second-in-command. You need favor to weather the seasons you go through. As you surrender more of yourself to serve someone else's dream, it's easy to get lost. Temptations, like seductive wives and all they represent, come up to distract you.

To keep those temptations at bay and steward your character, you can do three quick things:

1. **Examine Your Motives:** One way to check your character is to examine the motives behind your actions. This involves asking yourself why you are doing something and whether your reasons align with your values and principles. For example, if you are helping someone, are you doing it because you genu-inely care about them and want to make a positive impact, or are you doing it to gain recognition or approval from others? Examining your motives can help you identify whether your actions are driven by selflessness and compassion or by self-ishness and ego.

2. **Evaluate Your Actions:** Another way to check your character is to evaluate your actions. This involves reflecting on how you treat others, how you handle challenges, and whether you are living in accordance with your values and principles. For example, are you treating others with kindness and respect, even when it's difficult? Are you staying true to your beliefs

and principles, even when it's unpopular or inconvenient? Evaluating your actions can help you identify areas where you may need to improve and make changes.

3. **Be Exceptional:** The third way to check your character is to strive to be exceptional in everything you do. This means setting high standards for yourself and working to exceed them. It means being honest, trustworthy, and dependable, even when it's difficult. It means treating others with kindness and respect, even when they don't deserve it. Being exceptional requires a commitment to excellence and a willingness to go above and beyond what is expected. By striving to be exceptional, you can build a reputation for integrity, excellence, and character.

Joseph's character was intact, yet he still had another setback. That's life. There are so many times when we are accused, lied about, or attacked simply for the position we hold. When you're assigned to a leader you're often attacked by arrows aimed at them. Joseph was off to jail. Now what? His proximity pulled him to the prison.

> **When you're assigned to a leader you're often attacked by arrows aimed at them.**

When I was serving Bishop Abney, it became clear that I was to be the next senior leader of his church. As he got ready to retire, there were expectations and conversations that I would succeed him. Honestly, I didn't want the role because I didn't feel like it was mine to fill. But as the moment inched closer, I became increasingly excited about the opportunity.

Suddenly, I was fired from my role. I was starting to see a trend. What seemed like the prime moment in my career turned out to be an unexpected departure to my own personal prison. This wasn't exactly the same as Joseph's story, but the feeling of floating and then crashing to the ground—again—was becoming my new normal.

How are we supposed to process unexpected losses when we believe we are aligned with God's purpose for our lives? We recover from bad situations and redirect our lives, but then suddenly, we are reinjured in the most vulnerable places.

As Joseph ascended the ranks to run Potiphar's household, I imagine he felt less like hired help and more like family—just as I was family, literally, to Bishop Abney. That made the separation even more intense. While physically I was free, I became a prison to my thoughts. I hid away from the world out of embarrassment and pain. Many churches and organizations sought after me to solve their problems, but I couldn't fathom joining them.

A person's character speaks for itself. When you have done the work to steward it well, your reputation precedes you. Your reputation as a leader is what makes so many opportunities available to you. Joseph's story lets us know that not every opportunity is a good opportunity. People will attempt to poach you for their purposes, leaving you in the aftermath of their pursuits.

In conclusion, it is important to remember that adversity is a part of life, and everyone has to face it at some point. However, it is our response to adversity that determines the outcome of any situation. Joseph, in that season with Potiphar's wife, remained faithful to God despite the challenges he faced and was able to overcome temptation.

After my divorce and redemption, I learned to overcome by staying faithful to God. I believe we can find safety, favor, and success by trusting in God, even when things seem to be falling apart.

God wastes nothing that happens.

I can't tell you that a prison season isn't a necessary step in your leadership journey. I don't know where I would be without mine. But I can attest that God wastes nothing that happens. He takes things that work against you and makes them work for you. What are you doing to remain seated and secure in His plan for you?

CHAPTER 5

SITTING WITH YOURSELF

GENESIS 39:20-23
AND 40:1-23

"If at first you don't succeed, dust yourself off, and try again."[5] Those are not just popular song lyrics; they're a homily for life. If leadership and life have taught me anything, it's that evolution is constant. The world doesn't stop to have a pity party with you.

> **When you are in a prison state of mind, you have no choice but to sit with yourself.**

5 Aaliyah, vocalist, "Try Again," by Timothy Mosley and Stephen Garrett, released March 21, 2000, Lead single, *Romeo Must Die* Soundtrack, Blackground and Virgin Records.

When you are in a prison state of mind, you have no choice but to sit with yourself. Unlike the pit, where you are focused on simply surviving, the prison makes you long for the freedom you once had. As people walk in and out, you begin to fall into a deep state of comparison. *Why did this happen to me? Why can't I be released? I'm innocent in all this.*

Perhaps, this moment is one of the most defining leadership moments we experience as second-in-command leaders because if you can be seated and serve in this space, you can do anything anywhere. It's like a proving ground for your capabilities.

I was watching a video podcast about a man who became a leader in prison. He ran a multimillion-dollar operation in a federal penitentiary. The fascinating part of his story was his thought process. Before entering prison, he wasn't aware of all the skills he had. Something about confinement forces a person to become creative. You learn how much you can impact the world around you because you have no other options. The gentleman in the interview said he had time to observe how broken the system was, so he could insert himself and fix it. What a powerful statement. After prison, he knew he could apply what he learned to any activity he participated in. Now he makes millions of dollars a year and teaches others to do the same.

Confinement forces a person to become creative.

DR. JERMONE T. GLENN

What can leaders do when they feel confined? How do you feel when you are supposed to be living out your dream, but none of the pieces seem to be coming together? You may not be facing a literal prison, but you don't have all the resources you need. What if you have the money but no team? What if you have all the people in the world but no credit or money to build? Are you stuck in a job but have a passion that could pull you out if you only had the chance to focus on it? That sounds like a jail to me.

So many leaders, especially those serving other leaders, feel this never-ending tension. So what do you do? While prison may not be the palace you imagined ruling and reigning from, it is the perfect place to take your seat.

When I was fired from Bishop Abney's church, I was in a bad place. It got to the point that I didn't want to celebrate simple holidays. I avoided people like the plague. There were so many rumors and so many naysayers. The humiliation was blatant. The people who served with me were now serving the final blow against me.

I was afraid that my wife wouldn't choose me. She came from church royalty. She didn't *need* me, but she *chose* me. And to sit in her seat, no matter what was changing at the table, is a powerful metaphor for how we should remain in position no matter what.

While so many things were happening, it was her grandmother who had favor for me and wouldn't let me give up on everything. She pushed Erica and me together and provided wisdom and insight when I needed it the most. Grandma Abney has always been a powerhouse, but for some reason, this was an unexpected gift during a prison season in my life.

I often reflect on what Joseph's experience must have been like too. As we know, Joseph was a favored son of his father, Jacob, and was gifted with the ability to interpret dreams. However, his brothers grew jealous of him and sold him into slavery in Egypt. Despite this setback, Joseph managed to rise to a position of prominence in his new master's household, but he soon found himself unjustly accused of a crime he did not commit and thrown into prison.

The conditions in an ancient Egyptian prison were harsh. The prison itself was a dark and foreboding place with no natural light. Prisoners were held in dank underground cells or in spaces built into the walls of buildings. With little or no ventilation, the air was thick with the stench of despair and hopelessness. Prisoners were often subjected to forced labor, physical abuse, and brutal treatment, including torture and execution.

Despite the difficult circumstances, Joseph managed to find a glimmer of hope in the darkness. Scripture explains it like this:

> But while Joseph was there in the prison, the Lord was with him; he showed him kindness and granted him favor in the eyes of the prison warden. So the warden put Joseph in charge of all those held in the prison, and he was made responsible for all that was done there. The warden paid no attention to anything under Joseph's care, because the Lord was with Joseph and gave him success in whatever he did. —Genesis 39:20-23

Think about this for a second. The people meant to control him used no power over him. The authorities known for ruthless actions and treacherous behavior respected him. Favor can't be faked, but it can be grown. I believe this is because Joseph was himself functioning in his authenticity no matter what seat he took.

Favor can't be faked.

The thing about a seat is you have to take it. It doesn't matter where it is. When you go to a wedding, you sit where you are assigned. And while you are there, it's your opportunity to make the most of it. When the event is over, the seat doesn't matter anymore, but the impression you made in that seat can make all the difference for you. That's what we see in the next part of Joseph's story:

> Some time later, the cupbearer and the baker of the king of Egypt offended their master, the king of Egypt. Pharaoh was angry with his two officials, the chief cupbearer and the chief baker, and put them in custody in the house of the captain of the guard, in the same prison where Joseph was confined. The captain of the guard assigned them to Joseph, and he attended them.
>
> After they had been in custody for some time, each of the two men—the cupbearer and the baker of the king of Egypt, who were being held in prison—had a dream the same night, and each dream had a meaning of its own.
>
> When Joseph came to them the next morning, he saw that they were dejected. So he asked Pharaoh's officials who were in custody with him in his master's house, "Why do you look so sad today?"

"We both had dreams," they answered, "but there is no one to interpret them."

Then Joseph said to them, "Do not interpretations belong to God? Tell me your dreams."

So the chief cupbearer told Joseph his dream. He said to him, "In my dream I saw a vine in front of me, and on the vine were three branches. As soon as it budded, it blossomed, and its clusters ripened into grapes. Pharaoh's cup was in my hand, and I took the grapes, squeezed them into Pharaoh's cup and put the cup in his hand."

"This is what it means," Joseph said to him. "The three branches are three days. Within three days Pharaoh will lift up your head and restore you to your position, and you will put Pharaoh's cup in his hand, just as you used to do when you were his cupbearer. But when all goes well with you, remember me and show me kindness; mention me to Pharaoh and get me out of this prison. I was forcibly carried off from the land of the Hebrews, and even here I have done nothing to deserve being put in a dungeon."

When the chief baker saw that Joseph had given a favorable interpretation, he said to Joseph, "I too had a dream: On my head were three baskets of bread. In the top basket were all kinds of baked goods for Pharaoh, but the birds were eating them out of the basket on my head."

"This is what it means," Joseph said. "The three baskets are three days. Within three days Pharaoh will lift off your *head and impale your body on a pole. And the birds will eat away your flesh."*

Now the third day was Pharaoh's birthday, and he gave a feast for all his officials. He lifted up the heads of the chief cupbearer and the chief baker in the presence of his officials: He restored the chief cupbearer to his position, so that he once again put the cup into Pharaoh's hand—but he impaled the chief baker, just as Joseph had said to them in his interpretation.

The chief cupbearer, however, did not remember Joseph; he forgot him. —Genesis 40:1-23

So, you mean to tell me you can do everything right and be successful and still imprisoned? Exactly. We see that in Joseph's jail encounters. Joseph was basically the governor of the prison with everything he needed—except his freedom. He served from his seat every day, giving to the people, only to be reminded of his condition as they came in and out of prison. He used his gift of interpreting dreams to help two fellow prisoners who each had had a troubling dream. Joseph correctly interpreted the dreams, and one of the prisoners was eventually released and restored to his former position.

However, Joseph remained in prison, and it seemed as though he would be there indefinitely. It was a challenging time for him. I'm sure he struggled to maintain his faith and hope in the face of such adversity. But he did not give up.

SOWING SEEDS

After a while, my wife and I began to think about the things that we could do to impact the kingdom of God from Grand Rapids. We knew that we could assimilate into a new church like nothing had ever happened. People connected to us start praying too. They brought their tithes to our house. They put a demand on our next season. They brought us their dreams for the future. God was pulling us to build. That recurring theme came up repeatedly in our lives.

So we built The Revolution. For the record, The Revolution was never a prison for me, but it was built during a time when I felt confined. With the blessing of our leader and grandfather, we built up the ministry. We went from sixteen members who started with us to impacting thousands of people across the city every week.

A mentor of mine told me Grand Rapids was a testing ground. I know that in my spirit, but I wasn't aware that physical concepts and products were tested and incubated spiritually first. If you could get something to thrive in this system, it could thrive anywhere. Suddenly, our experiences made sense.

We were able to do things that had never been done. From the beginning, I gave everyone leadership power in our church. We turned the church into full productions before it was popular. We live-streamed services across the country when people thought it was sacrilegious. The Revolution was a space where people entered and catapulted into destiny. Some of the biggest worship leaders and pastors had encounters at The Revolution before they were propelled into some of the most significant places in their lives.

In many ways, The Revolution itself was a system for interpreting dreams. Through mentorship programs, leadership development, and relationship training, we got to do anything and everything we set forth to do. I had an amazing staff and volunteer staff that helped me steer the church the way God led us.

We did this for fourteen years, and it felt like it was the dream. I was doing everything I saw. We were surrounded by the most incredible congregation. We raised mentees that became family. We birthed babies, married couples, counseled the lost, and healed the sick, but I kept feeling there was more. I kept feeling like I was a caged eagle.

> **How you serve people in low places qualifies you for high places.**

Remember that I told you a prison season is pivotal for your process. It's the ultimate testing for your skills, but it also puts a demand on your identity. Who are you as a leader? How you serve people in low places qualifies you for high places. If Joseph had belittled the prisoners, he wouldn't have made it to the palace.

If I hadn't given everything to The Revolution, who would I be? If you don't give *everything* to the spaces and places God calls you to lead, your results will be disastrous.

God began to give me a glimpse of what I prayed for in private places:

- » Impacting the nations.
- » Going from local to global.
- » Using the internet to further the kingdom.
- » Innovating the church gathering into an experience of transformation.
- » Starting a movement to mobilize people for maximum results.

These things weren't just sayings in our church; they were in our DNA. We could feel a shift, but if I'm real, I sometimes felt forgotten in my small city.

SEEMINGLY FORGOTTEN

Joseph waited to be remembered. He'd done so much. He served in his suffering. He was honorable and upright before God. Yet he still felt forgotten.

This is why so many people don't take their seat when it's time. The pain of being forgotten is too real, and they're not willing to risk it. Unfortunately, though, both pain and purpose are part of the process. They go together to produce the whole. I know what it's like to give up a piece of yourself to fit into someone else's puzzle. I understand how you can lead and still feel lost.

As leaders who serve other leaders, there is always the feeling that something is missing. You are forgotten. You solved the problem for everyone else, but who is there to solve it for you? Who is your number two? Who's going to make sure everything is okay for your family? You spend all day driving people around; who drives you home? That can't be the way that it's supposed to be!

Leaders are drowning because they haven't learned the lessons that come in a prison season. Prison is a waiting space, and if we can keep that mentality, we can be fulfilled and content—even there.

Master Every Moment

Spoiler alert! Joseph got out of prison, but he would have never gotten out of prison if he hadn't learned to master and maximize every moment that was given to him. As leaders, it's always our responsibility to be ready, so we don't have to get ready. Joseph exemplified this. When it's our turn to be called upon, we have to be ready to answer the call. However, a lot of times, we get caught in the trap and mentality that we have to reserve our best for our biggest moments. That is a setup to get you to fall on your face publicly because you have not operated privately in your gifting. When you live in reality and with the mindset that you have the opportunity to maximize and master every moment, success will follow you.

> **Be ready, so you don't have to get ready.**

Success followed Joseph everywhere he went. It's clear in the text that he was favored at home. He was favored among slave traders. He was favored to be at Potiphar's house. Then, ultimately, he became a favorite in the prison system. He ran the entire prison because he knew how to master the moment.

When Potiphar's wife was coming after him, he turned away because he knew that wouldn't exemplify what God had called him to do. What about you? What about us? We must master every moment because every moment is a seed, and we get to choose the seeds that we sow. As I told you before, you have to eat the harvest of your seeds.

So when you get the opportunity to serve someone, serve with all that's in you. Whether you're serving somebody who seems to be in a low position or you are prophesying to kings, it's your ability to master the minor moments that allows you to win in the major ones.

Every Seat is Significant

"One day" is the enemy of progress. It's also the saboteur of purpose. You can't *one day* walk in purpose because that's disconnecting your destiny from the decisions that you are making right now, and they are all connected. Every season of your life is the succession of the previous season. Your future is decided by your present actions.

My seat as a janitor was no less significant than my seat as senior pastor of The Revolution or as the executive pastor of a megachurch today. Every seat that God had guided me to was a place for me to be who He calls me to be. We get too hung up on hierarchy, positional leadership, and on the prize that comes with power. But leadership wasn't instituted to plow over people. It was instituted for the people, meaning that when we consider everyone to be leaders, no one seat becomes more important than the other.

Jesus is in the most significant seat at the right hand of the Father. So as leaders, if we use that knowledge to shift our paradigms, we become more powerful. We recognize that every other seat is the same. If you watch political shows, I'm sure you've heard the phrase, "I serve at the pleasure." That's what our seats are: an opportunity for God to rule and reign through us wherever we go. They are for us to bring the kingdom to a specific space.

Joseph modeled that in every situation—from the pit to the prison—and, ultimately, we shall see it happen in the palace too. Let me tell you a secret: every single seat is significant, or it wouldn't exist.

> **Every single seat is significant, or it wouldn't exist.**

There are simply too many facets of life that require leadership for there to be only one leader. This is very clear in our society. There are boards made up of many directors. The Supreme Court consists of nine justices. There are fifteen executive departments within the US government, and each of them has hundreds of leadership roles. When one of those positions goes vacant, they fill it because the seat matters.

The truth is it's not about the seat but about who sits in it. That's what truly adds value to every space. So as a leader who serves other leaders, let me save you some time and struggle by affirming that you add value every place that you go.

Don't Forfeit Your Seat

If you don't master those first two lessons, there is a high probability that you will forfeit your seat entirely. You'll miss it because you're mad at the circumstances. Don't allow the environment you're in to determine what can be extracted from you. Many times, people who are second-in-command can feel taken advantage of. You can feel as if you give and give and give but never receive. You go above and beyond without recognition, but if you don't learn to be content in that space, I guarantee that you won't keep it very long.

Seats are simply assignments. God gives you grace for your assignment, but if you choose not to fulfill it, I believe the grace is lifted. The lesson in this is to understand that we have a responsibility and a choice to take our seats. Understand this: our posture permits our promotion. God uses the available. If you are not available, meaning you don't show up and sit in your seat when you're supposed to be there, you'll be considered absent. And if you are absent in one season, you forfeit the ability to show up in the next. If Joseph had never interpreted the dreams of the chief baker and the chief cupbearer, he would have been disqualified from interpreting Pharaoh's dream.

We are no different. We know that God is no respecter of persons. Therefore, we can take the same principle and apply it to our lives. Don't forfeit your seat in the future because you don't like the table that you're sitting at now. I started in one of the seemingly lowest seats there could be, and time and time again, God's favor promoted me. I believe He'll do the same for you.

Interpreting Someone Else's Dream Is Part of the Kingdom Economy

We don't know how many dreams Joseph interpreted, but we can imagine that it wasn't only the few that we read about. The truth is that being able to insert yourself in somebody else's dream and pull out the God themes is the way that the economy of the kingdom works. Helping someone achieve their dreams aligns you for your assignment. From the beginning, I explained to my team that the second man is the most powerful man. The leader has the vision; the second-in-command has the opportunity to innovate and execute that dream in unique ways.

> **Helping someone achieve their dreams aligns you for your assignment.**

We live in an interdependent culture. Everyone is helping someone fulfill their dreams. When I decided to birth a church, my wife left her job to help me build that dream. When she wanted to start a boutique, I was right beside her, picking out items from vendors around the country.

When my children have a dream, I become the dream developer. The reality for all leaders is to understand that God trusts you to have influence and make an impact from the seat He's assigned to you in this season. I know that society has groomed us to all be go-getters, out for ourselves and our families. But I will tell you this. You cannot be sown into if you do not sow up.

> **You cannot be sown into if you do not sow up.**

At this point in my ministry, I have been beyond blessed to have people not only submit themselves to my leadership but invest their time in my life. Sons and daughters have come alongside me to help me fulfill the mission and vision God has given me. I didn't stop sowing because they were sowing into me. As a senior pastor, I had a pastor, and I still help my pastor build his dreams. I tie into him because I understand the kingdom economy.

Seed time and harvest is a concept that is true for each of us. What you give, you will get back. Don't waste time giving from a place of bitterness because you will be better with what you receive back. Instead, I challenge every leader to invest their best into someone else's dream and watch how God blows their mind with what He invests into theirs.

We Exist to Serve Other People

It's irresponsible for us to waste time grumbling about serving someone else when all of humanity exists to do just that. That's it. That's the lesson right there.

But seriously, have you ever heard the phrase "Die empty." It's the ideology that you don't waste an idea. You execute all that God has shown you, and so much of what you're called to execute has nothing to do with you. We're afraid to give away our ideas because we think that we have to monetize everything. To become millionaires, we think we must hoard our thoughts, systems, and processes, but that is the poorest mindset that you can have. When you give is when you receive.

Giving your ideas does not deplete you; it puts a demand on you to receive more. I believe that God will not leave you on empty. When Joseph interpreted the chief cupbearer's and the chief baker's dreams, it did not take away any of his abilities. If anything, it sharpened them. Therefore, when Pharaoh called upon Joseph, he was prepared to do what he'd always done.

Joseph put himself out there to serve other people. When he went to check on his brothers, he was going to serve them. In Potiphar's house, he became in charge of everything because he served. The same was repeated in prison. In fact, I believe that one of the reasons God chose, trusted, and utilized Joseph during a time of great famine in Egypt was because Joseph's heart was to serve people. He could not have done that if he was focused on self-preservation because self-preservation causes you to be stingy.

Service requires you to sacrifice. That's why Joseph is a type and shadow of Christ. Joseph modeled the servant's heart. He modeled being a light in dark places. Ultimately, through his obedience, he saved an entire people. Joseph was not just a seed—he was a first fruit.

He's an example of how all leaders should carry themselves in their interactions with others. Our primary objective is to serve.

We serve God by serving others.

While you focus on learning the lessons, it doesn't change the fact that people forget. But God doesn't. He never forgets you or what you've done. You can focus on Him and allow Him to focus on everything around you. Serve Him by serving others.

My challenge to you is to go back to your dream, think about what you need to fulfill it, and then go and be that for someone else. That is the key to unlocking reciprocity in your leadership journey and life. How can you use that key to open one more door to your destiny?

CHAPTER 6

SHARING YOUR GIFTS
GENESIS 41:1-40

When Pharaoh himself had a troubling dream, the former prisoner whom Joseph had helped remembered him and recommended him to Pharaoh. Joseph was summoned from prison and brought before Pharaoh who asked him to interpret the dream.

Joseph's interpretation proved to be correct, and Pharaoh was so impressed that he made Joseph his second-in-command, giving him authority over all of Egypt. Joseph was finally able to use his gift to help others as he managed the country's resources during a time of great famine.

In many ways, Joseph's journey from Potiphar's house to prison and eventually to a position of power is a story of resilience and determination. He never gave up, even in the darkest of times, and he continued to hold on to his faith and his belief in a better future.

The story of Joseph also raises important questions about the nature of punishment and justice in ancient Egypt. Prisons were primarily used for detaining people who were awaiting trial or punishment as well as for holding prisoners of war. Punishment was the primary goal, but purpose was Joseph's reward.

> **Punishment was the primary goal, but purpose was Joseph's reward.**

PHARAOH'S DREAMS

When two full years had passed, Pharaoh had a dream: He was standing by the Nile, when out of the river there came up seven cows, sleek and fat, and they grazed among the reeds. After them, seven other cows, ugly and gaunt, came up out of the Nile and stood beside those on the riverbank. And the cows that were ugly and gaunt ate up the seven sleek, fat cows. Then Pharaoh woke up.

He fell asleep again and had a second dream: Seven heads of grain, healthy and good, were growing on a single stalk. After them, seven other heads of grain sprouted—thin and scorched by

DR. JERMONE T. GLENN

the east wind. The thin heads of grain swallowed up the seven healthy, full heads. Then Pharaoh woke up; it had been a dream.

In the morning his mind was troubled, so he sent for all the magicians and wise men of Egypt. Pharaoh told them his dreams, but no one could interpret them for him.

Then the chief cupbearer said to Pharaoh, "Today I am reminded of my shortcomings. Pharaoh was once angry with his servants, and he imprisoned me and the chief baker in the house of the captain of the guard. Each of us had a dream the same night, and each dream had a meaning of its own. Now a young Hebrew was there with us, a servant of the captain of the guard. We told him our dreams, and he interpreted them for us, giving each man the interpretation of his dream. And things turned out exactly as he interpreted them to us: I was restored to my position, and the other man was impaled."

So Pharaoh sent for Joseph, and he was quickly brought from the dungeon. When he had shaved and changed his clothes, he came before Pharaoh.

Pharaoh said to Joseph, "I had a dream, and no one can interpret it. But I have heard it said of you that when you hear a dream you can interpret it."

"I cannot do it," Joseph replied to Pharaoh, "but God will give Pharaoh the answer he desires."

Then Pharaoh said to Joseph, "In my dream I was standing on the bank of the Nile, when out of the river there came up seven cows, fat and sleek, and they grazed among the reeds. After them, seven other cows came up—scrawny and very ugly and lean. I had never seen such ugly cows in all the land of Egypt. The lean, ugly cows ate up the seven fat cows that came up first. But even after they ate them, no one could tell that they had done so; they looked just as ugly as before. Then I woke up.

"In my dream I saw seven heads of grain, full and good, growing on a single stalk. After them, seven other heads sprouted—withered and thin and scorched by the east wind. The thin heads of grain swallowed up the seven good heads. I told this to the magicians, but none of them could explain it to me."

Joseph said to Pharaoh, "The dreams of Pharaoh are one and the same. God has revealed to Pharaoh what he is about to do. The seven good cows are seven years, and the seven good heads of grain are seven years; it is one and the same dream. The seven lean, ugly cows that came up afterward are seven years, and so are the seven worthless heads of grain scorched by the east wind: They are seven years of famine.

"It is just as I said to Pharaoh: God has shown Pharaoh what he is about to do. Seven years of great abundance are coming throughout the land of Egypt, but seven years of famine will follow them. Then all the abundance in Egypt will be forgotten, and the famine will ravage the land. The abundance in the land will not be remembered, because the famine that follows it will be so severe. The reason the dream was given to Pharaoh in two forms is that the matter has been firmly decided by God, and God will do it soon.

"And now let Pharaoh look for a discerning and wise man and put him in charge of the land of Egypt. Let Pharaoh appoint commissioners over the land to take a fifth of the harvest of Egypt during the seven years of abundance. They should collect all the food of these good years that are coming and store up the grain under the authority of Pharaoh, to be kept in the cities for food. This food should be held in reserve for the country, to be used during the seven years of famine that will come upon Egypt, so that the country may not be ruined by the famine."

The plan seemed good to Pharaoh and to all his officials. So Pharaoh asked them, "Can we find anyone like this man, one in whom is the spirit of God?"

Then Pharaoh said to Joseph, "Since God has made all this known to you, there is no one so discerning and wise as you. You shall be in charge of my palace, and all my people are to submit to your orders. Only with respect to the throne will I be greater than you." —Genesis 41:1-40

Joseph went from prison to a place of organizing a strategy that single-handedly would save many nations. Whew! This took everything he had learned and compounded it into a system. Joseph served the rich at Potiphar's. He served the poor in prison. He lead both from the palace.

From being sold into slavery at the age of seventeen until reaching his position as a high-ranking official in Egypt around the age of thirty, Joseph was being groomed for this work. He may not have realized it, but this new role was leading him right into the dream he had all along.

> **Joseph served the rich at Potiphar's.**
> **He served the poor in prison.**
> **He lead both from the palace.**

SACRIFICING AS A SERVICE

In 2019, I could feel that we were on the precipice of something earth-shattering as a church. My wife began to sense it too. We prayed, fasted, gathered our leaders, and asked God what He was doing. At one point, we gathered all of the intercessors from our church and gave the church back to God. He told my wife that we needed to let it go. We thought that it was a seed. He was going to show us how to restructure, and He would give it back to us in a way that was better than we had ever imagined.

In August, I went to visit my long-time ministry brother Pastor John Hannah. Through a series of events that are cataloged in another book, God revealed that I was to join Pastor Hannah at New Life Covenant Church Southeast in Chicago. That was a piece of shattering news for our church. We would become part of the New Life community and be a satellite campus in Grand Rapids. The leaders I had in place at my church would continue running the daily operations. We would conduct satellite services by broadcasting one of the services from Chicago into the Grand Rapids sanctuary.

People thought I was insane for the idea. The way they dragged our name through the mud, determinedly undermined our character, and made fun of our ideas was outrageous, but many times, a lack of vision can cause people to lose sight. We knew—my wife and I—that God was calling us to Chicago, but we also felt an extreme pull to stay connected to our congregation in Grand Rapids.

I imagine that promotion and swift change are hard for every leader. While you are extremely excited about the opportunity before you, you are also immersed in grief and guilt about what you're leaving behind. I was no different, and to some extent, I believe that Joseph missed the people that he was leaving behind. However, I know he was ready to get out of prison.

Every seat requires a sacrifice.

Some of us would rather stay in the prison system out of fear than pursue the new opportunities that God places before us. Every seat requires a sacrifice. Giving up senior leadership and what I had created at The Revolution was my sacrifice.

People have many questions about our arrangement: How do we make it work? What's it like to go from a senior to an executive pastor? But the truth is I have *always* served somebody else's dream.

Ultimately, we're all serving God's dream. Leading for someone else does not diminish you. It diversifies your ability to serve in multiple capacities. I still have my ministry, and part of my ministry is to be an executive pastor at New Life.

Being second-in-command is the most strategic position that you can be in. It means that you have been ordained as a dream developer. You are a divine agent of execution. God takes help seriously. In fact, in Genesis, when He created the woman, He referred to her as the help, but the word that He used—*ezer*—is a word that He also used to refer to Himself. It is God-like to serve somebody else.

However, it is not going to happen if you're unwilling to give up something of your own. We released The Revolution back to God. We believed that we had a way to stay connected, but it wasn't what our city believed they needed at the time. So we had some choices to make: Did my family continue to stay stuck between two places? Did I continue to drive to Chicago every Thursday, live without my family until Sunday evening, and drive back to Grand Rapids? I couldn't. So, after nine months of back and forth, it was time to disconnect. Then COVID-19 happened. No one was in the building, and it showed me that it could work. I think that made the sacrifice even more rewarding.

What are you willing to give up for an imminent reward in God's kingdom?

CHAPTER 7

SERVING YOUR SEAT

GENESIS 41:41-57

When Joseph introduced his strategy for resource management, the other leaders could've tried to stop him, but they were in unfamiliar territory. No one could interpret Pharaoh's dream correctly, let alone develop a system of sustainability. But that is exactly what Joseph did, and Pharaoh let him implement it:

> So Pharaoh said to Joseph, "I hereby put you in charge of the whole land of Egypt." Then Pharaoh took his signet ring from his finger and put it on Joseph's finger. He dressed him in robes of fine linen and put a gold chain around his neck. He had him ride in a chariot as his second-in-command, and people shouted before him, "Make way!" Thus he put him in charge of the whole land of Egypt.

Then Pharaoh said to Joseph, "I am Pharaoh, but without your word no one will lift hand or foot in all Egypt." Pharaoh gave Joseph the name Zaphenath-Paneah and gave him Asenath daughter of Potiphera, priest of On, to be his wife. And Joseph went throughout the land of Egypt.

Joseph was thirty years old when he entered the service of Pharaoh king of Egypt. And Joseph went out from Pharaoh's presence and traveled throughout Egypt. During the seven years of abundance the land produced plentifully. Joseph collected all the food produced in those seven years of abundance in Egypt and stored it in the cities. In each city he put the food grown in the fields surrounding it. Joseph stored up huge quantities of grain, like the sand of the sea; it was so much that he stopped keeping records because it was beyond measure.

Before the years of famine came, two sons were born to Joseph by Asenath daughter of Potiphera, priest of On. Joseph named his firstborn Manasseh and said, "It is because God has made me forget all my trouble and all my father's household." The second son he named Ephraim and said, "It is because God has made me fruitful in the land of my suffering."

The seven years of abundance in Egypt came to an end, and the seven years of famine began, just as Joseph had said. There was famine in all the other lands, but in the whole land of Egypt there was food. When all Egypt began to feel the famine, the people cried to Pharaoh for food. Then Pharaoh told all the Egyptians, "Go to Joseph and do what he tells you."

When the famine had spread over the whole country, Joseph opened all the storehouses and sold grain to the Egyptians, for the famine was severe throughout Egypt. And all the world came to Egypt to buy grain from Joseph, because the famine was severe everywhere. —Genesis 41:41–57

Joseph utilized every skill he'd cultivated in Potiphar's household and those damp, dismal dungeons. He had spent approximately thirteen years as a slave—from around when he was seventeen and telling his family about his dream—until he was thirty when Pharaoh made him second-in-command. God didn't waste a moment of Joseph's suffering. And because he was willing to be used by God, he averted what could have been a calamity for the kingdom of Egypt and the surrounding nations. Times were lean; make no mistake. However, many were saved that otherwise would have experienced the slow, painful death of starvation.

Today, I am utilizing every skill that was cultivated before this moment to forward the kingdom agenda on the earth. Leadership development is one of my top priorities, and I get to do that at New Life. Marriage ministry is essential for my wife and me; we get to live that here. However, I would be dishonest if I said that the growing pains of two leaders coming together were nonexistent. As we merge our two styles, a congregation making space to receive somebody else is challenging.

> **When following God is a priority He will position you in seats of unprecedented possibility.**

Only you can determine if your sacrifice is worth the seat that you will take. When following God is a priority He will position you in seats of unprecedented possibility. How do you manage that? How do you stop feeling like a failure because your dream didn't work in one season? Now you're serving somebody else—doing the same thing—in this season. That doesn't make your sacrifice a personal punishment. You didn't fail! Dreams often just look different from how we originally perceive them.

This is something that I have to learn and live out every week. Even after years of being at New Life, I still understand that this was a sacrifice not only for me but my family and all the people connected to us.

But God placed me here at the perfect time. Pastor Hannah and I often talk about what the pandemic did to the church. It forced us to change methods and not just manage the routines. Being an innovator and executor, it was necessary that I come at that moment. I already had experience streaming church, so when Pastor Hannah had a dream of reaching people during the pandemic, I had the interpretation of his dream and the skills to execute it already.

It was just like Joseph. His skill was necessary for his moment in Egypt. When God pulls you into any space of leadership, know that it's because you are needed at that moment so that you can understand what God wants to do and expand it on the earth.

FORMULA FOR SUCCESS

Joseph was prepared, and the strategy that he used can ensure that any second-in-command leader is successful in their role.

See the Problem

Seeing problems around us is not merely a skill; it's a crucial mindset that sets successful leaders apart from the rest. It's about having a sharp sense of awareness and the ability to respond to situations effectively.

Leaders who possess the ability to identify problems and challenges can create a culture of excellence in their organizations. They empower their teams to focus on finding solutions rather than dwelling on the obstacles that hold them back.

To cultivate this mindset, leaders must develop several skill sets. First and foremost, they must be excellent communicators. Leaders must create an environment where everyone feels heard, valued, and respected. They must encourage open dialogue, constructive feedback, and healthy debate, which fosters an innovative and creative culture.

Leaders must also possess strong critical thinking and problem-solving skills. They must analyze situations and take into account different perspectives, weighing the pros and cons of various solutions. They must be open to feedback and willing to learn from their mistakes.

Another essential skill for leaders is emotional intelligence. They must be able to understand and manage their own emotions and those of others. Leaders who can create a positive and supportive work environment build trust and loyalty among their team, leading to increased engagement and productivity.

This is crucial for gaining influence and becoming better leaders. When we demonstrate the ability to identify issues before they become major problems, we show our teams that we are proactive and have a strong sense of situational awareness.

By proactively addressing problems, we also build trust with our teams. They begin to see us as capable and reliable leaders who have their best interests in mind. This trust and respect are critical for gaining influence, as it allows us to effectively communicate our vision and motivate our teams toward a common goal.

Additionally, when we demonstrate our problem-solving skills and ability to respond quickly and efficiently, we inspire confidence in our teams. This confidence leads to greater job satisfaction and higher levels of productivity, as employees feel empowered to tackle challenges and contribute to the success of the organization.

Ultimately, the ability to see problems around us and respond properly is a fundamental skill set for any leader. By developing this skill, we not only become better leaders but also gain influence and build a stronger, more motivated team.

Speak the Truth

In speaking truth to Pharaoh, Joseph demonstrated his skill in problem-solving and strategic thinking. He also showed his ability to communicate difficult truths in a way that Pharaoh could understand and act upon. By providing a concrete plan of action, Joseph gained Pharaoh's trust and was put in charge of overseeing the implementation of the plan. Ultimately, Joseph's truth-speaking and leadership helped save Egypt from the devastating effects of the famine.

> **Speaking the truth to power positions you to be trusted.**

Speaking the truth to power positions you to be trusted. By providing honest feedback and insight into the problems and challenges facing the organization, leaders are able to make informed decisions and take decisive action.

This type of transparency can save time by cutting through the noise and identifying the root causes of issues. When leaders are able to quickly understand what's happening, they can take swift action to address problems before they become bigger issues. This not only saves time but also prevents the need for reactive crisis management, which can be costly and disruptive.

Additionally, leaders who are willing to hear and act on the truth gain the trust and respect of their team. When employees feel that their concerns and opinions are valued, they are more likely to be engaged and committed to their work. This can lead to improved collaboration, innovation, and productivity.

Furthermore, when leaders model a culture of transparency and honesty, it can set the tone for the entire organization. Employees are more likely to follow suit and communicate openly and honestly with one another, leading to better problem-solving and decision-making at all levels of the organization.

Staff Your Weakness

Pharaoh gave Joseph what he needed to get the job done. The Bible doesn't explicitly say, but I know that managing people is a large part of accomplishing anything. It's important to staff teams. Know whom you need before your leader becomes involved. Identify what skills you need and who could possibly fill them. One pitfall of second-in-command leadership is feeling like you have to accomplish everything by yourself. You probably can, but it will be better if you trust other people. Initiate and then delegate.

As a leader, it's essential to be self-aware and recognize your weaknesses. Once you identify your weaknesses, you can work to staff them by finding team members or collaborators who have strengths in those areas. For example, if you're not skilled in project management, you can seek out team members who are excellent project managers to help manage and organize projects.

Collaboration is also key in accomplishing a vision. When you have a shared vision, you can delegate tasks to individuals based on their strengths, which allows for a more efficient and effective work environment. Leaders should aim to build a team that complements each other's strengths and weaknesses to achieve the vision.

DR. JERMONE T. GLENN

It's also essential to communicate your weaknesses to your team openly. This helps to create a culture of transparency, which can encourage team members to speak up about their weaknesses and ask for help when needed. By being open about your weaknesses, you can also create opportunities for team members to step up and take on additional responsibilities, which can help them grow professionally.

Ultimately, build a competent team that compensates for your weakness and complements your strengths. This approach can foster a collaborative and supportive work environment where everyone feels valued, which can increase productivity and build trust.

> **Build a competent team that compensates for your weakness and complements your strengths.**

Secure a Structure

Joseph was in control of creating a system that would last for fourteen years. It couldn't be dependent on which people were around and which had moved on. He needed a system that could scale and be efficient, fair, and consistent.

If a system is designed in a way that it's dependent on specific individuals, it can limit the organization's ability to scale. As the organization grows, it may become more challenging to find and retain individuals who possess the same skills, knowledge, and experience required to perform the functions. By building a system that is not dependent on specific individuals, an organization can scale more easily.

A system that is dependent on individuals is not sustainable in the long run. People come and go, and if a critical person leaves, the system can break down. By building a system that isn't dependent on specific individuals, an organization can ensure that it can continue to function even if key individuals leave.

When a system is dependent on specific individuals, it may be slower because individuals may need to spend more time explaining how the system works to new hires or training others to perform the functions. By building a system that isn't dependent on specific individuals, an organization can be more efficient and save time.

A team may be subject to inconsistencies because different individuals may perform the same functions differently. By building a system that is independent of individuals, an organization can ensure that functions are performed consistently, regardless of who is performing them.

You need the same for your organization too.

Serve the Seat

Being second-in-command means anticipating the needs of the other leader. One of the primary responsibilities is to ensure that the senior leaders have everything they need to fulfill their responsibilities. This may involve managing the day-to-day operations of the organization, overseeing the implementation of strategies and initiatives, and supporting the senior leaders in their decision-making processes.

To ensure that the senior leadership gets everything they need, the second-in-command must possess excellent communication skills. They must actively listen to the needs of the senior leaders and be able to clearly communicate those needs to the rest of the team. It is essential to understand the goals and objectives of the organization and work collaboratively with others to ensure that those goals are achieved.

Another priority of the second-in-command is to build and maintain strong relationships with team members, stakeholders, and clients. This involves being approachable, responsive, and supportive. The second-in-command must lead by example, demonstrating integrity, accountability, and a strong work ethic. They must be willing to roll up their sleeves and work alongside team members to ensure that goals are met.

Ultimately, the role of the second-in-command is to support senior leadership in achieving the goals and objectives of the organization. This requires a strong focus on the needs of others and the ability to build and maintain strong relationships. By working collaboratively and communicating effectively, the second-in-command can help to ensure that the senior leadership has everything they need to lead the organization to success.

When Joseph did these things, not only was it assured that the people of Egypt would be sustained—but also people from other regions, including Joseph's own family. Joseph built a system that transformed critics to cheerleaders, and non-believers to benefactors. What would that look like for you?

> **Joseph built a system that transformed critics to cheerleaders, and non-believers to benefactors.**

DR. JERMONE T. GLENN

CHAPTER 8

SITTING TOGETHER

GENESIS 42 AND 43

A dream inside a dream is never diminished. It becomes incorporated into the future in a new way. As Joseph served Pharaoh, he would be standing right in the middle of a dream birthed in him years previously because in **Genesis 42**, the story of Joseph and his brothers continues:

> **A dream inside a dream is never diminished.**

When Jacob learned that there was grain in Egypt, he said to his sons, "Why do you just keep looking at each other?" He continued, "I have heard that there is grain in Egypt. Go down there and buy some for us, so that we may live and not die."

Then ten of Joseph's brothers went down to buy grain from Egypt. But Jacob did not send Benjamin, Joseph's brother, with the others, because he was afraid that harm might come to him. So Israel's sons were among those who went to buy grain, for there was famine in the land of Canaan also . . . .

When Joseph's brothers arrived, they bowed down to him with their faces to the ground. As soon as Joseph saw his brothers, he recognized them, but he pretended to be a stranger and spoke harshly to them. "Where do you come from?" he asked.

"From the land of Canaan," they replied, "to buy food."

Although Joseph recognized his brothers, they did not recognize him. Then he remembered his dreams about them and said to them, "You are spies! You have come to see where our land is unprotected."

. . . But they replied, "Your servants were twelve brothers, the sons of one man, who lives in the land of Canaan. The youngest is now with our father, and one is no more."

Joseph said to them, " . . . This is how you will be tested: As surely as Pharaoh lives, you will not leave this place unless your youngest brother comes here . . . . And he put them all in custody for three days.

On the third day, Joseph said to them, "Do this and you will live, for I fear God: If you are honest men, let one of your brothers

DR. JERMONE T. GLENN

stay here in prison, while the rest of you go and take grain back for your starving households. But you must bring your youngest brother to me, so that your words may be verified and that you may not die . . . ."

They said to one another, "Surely we are being punished because of our brother. We saw how distressed he was when he pleaded with us for his life, but we would not listen; that's why this distress has come on us."

Reuben replied, "Didn't I tell you not to sin against the boy! But you wouldn't listen! Now we must give an accounting for his blood." They did not realize that Joseph could understand them, since he was using an interpreter.

He turned away from them and began to weep, but then came back and spoke to them again. He had Simeon taken from them and bound before their eyes. —Genesis 42:1-24

Due to the unbearable conditions throughout the land caused by the famine, Jacob sent ten of his sons to Egypt to buy grain. Joseph, who was now a powerful official in Egypt, recognized his brothers when they arrived, but they did not recognize him. Needless to say, he didn't look anything like the young dreamer they had ridiculed and thrown into a pit over a decade before. And in that one encounter, Joseph's dream came to fruition: "When Joseph's brothers arrived, they bowed down to him with their faces to the ground" (Genesis 42:6). It must have been a surreal moment for Joseph. The ones who had ridiculed his dream—the vultures who had devoured his vision—took the knee, their faces to the ground, and assumed a subservient position.

How easy it would have been to confront them—to make them grovel further and beg for his forgiveness. Instead, Joseph decided to test his brothers to see if they had changed since they had sold him into slavery all those years ago. He accused them of being spies and imprisoned them for three days. On the third day, he released them and told them that he would keep one of them in Egypt while the rest returned home to get their youngest brother, Benjamin. All of this speaks to Joseph being significantly seated in his seat. He had the power to exact immediate revenge. But because he was reconciled in his own heart and mind that he was in the right place—exactly where he belonged—his perspective encompassed the bigger picture.

Joseph's perspective encompassed the bigger picture.

Joseph was also given the chance to see that his brothers were wracked with guilt over what they had done to him. They saw their current troubles as divine punishment for their past sins. Because of the seat in which Joseph sat—that of second-in-command in Egypt and a foreigner who required an interpreter because he supposedly didn't speak their language—they could talk freely among themselves. They didn't know that Joseph understood everything they were saying. They weren't in a position to manipulate Joseph by appealing to the bonds of brotherhood or the tenuous emotional health of their heartbroken father. They were simply ten brothers lamenting their hard hearts and treacherous treatment of the younger brother, who, in his distress, had pleaded for his life.

Joseph was also working to restore his family relationships. While Simeon was taken from them and again thrown in jail, the brothers agreed to bring Benjamin to Egypt. They were unsure how to explain this to their father, who was deeply attached to Benjamin—his only other child with Rachel—after losing Joseph, but Genesis 42 ends with the brothers returning to Canaan with the grain they "purchased" since Joseph had instructed that the men's gold also be placed in the bags of grain. The events of this chapter set the stage for the next, in which the brothers return to Egypt with Benjamin and face Joseph once again.

THE SECOND TRIP

Jacob and his sons ran out of food again, and reluctantly, because Joseph had warned the men that they would not see his face again unless their youngest brother was with them, Jacob agreed to send Benjamin to Egypt. This time, though, Jacob gave additional instructions to take some of the best products of the land with them as a gift for Pharaoh's second-in-command. The men, of course, had noticed that their silver had been returned, so Jacob also told them to take twice as much this time. And with these parting words, "Take your brother also and go back to the man at once. And may God Almighty grant you mercy before the man so that he will let your other brother and Benjamin come back with you. As for me, if I am bereaved, I am bereaved" (Genesis 43:13-14), the men left.

So the men took the gifts and ... hurried down to Egypt and presented themselves to Joseph. When Joseph saw Benjamin with them, he said to the steward of his house, "Take these men to my house, slaughter an animal and prepare a meal; they are to eat with me at noon."

The man did as Joseph told him and took the men to Joseph's house. Now the men were frightened when they were taken to his house....

[Thinking it was about the silver] they went up to Joseph's steward and spoke to him at the entrance to the house. "We beg your pardon, our lord," they said, "we came down here the first time to buy food. But at the place where we stopped for the night we opened our sacks and each of us found his silver—the exact weight—in the mouth of his sack. So we have brought it back with us. We have also brought additional silver with us to buy food. We don't know who put our silver in our sacks."

"It's all right," he said. "Don't be afraid. Your God, the God of your father, has given you treasure in your sacks; I received your silver." Then he brought Simeon out to them.

The steward took the men into Joseph's house, gave them water to wash their feet and provided fodder for their donkeys. They prepared their gifts for Joseph's arrival at noon, because they had heard that they were to eat there.

When Joseph came home, they presented to him the gifts they had brought into the house, and they bowed down before him

to the ground. He asked them how they were, and then he said,
"How is your aged father you told me about? Is he still living?"

They replied, "Your servant our father is still alive and well."
And they bowed down, prostrating themselves before him.

As he looked about and saw his brother Benjamin, his own
mother's son, he asked, "Is this your youngest brother, the one
you told me about?" And he said, "God be gracious to you, my
son." Deeply moved at the sight of his brother, Joseph hurried
out and looked for a place to weep. He went into his private
room and wept there.

After he had washed his face, he came out . . . .

The men had been seated before him in the order of their
ages, from the firstborn to the youngest; and they looked at each
other in astonishment. When portions were served to them from
Joseph's table, Benjamin's portion was five times as much as
anyone else's. So they feasted and drank freely with him. —Gen-
esis 43:15–31 and 33–34

Anxious about returning to Egypt, fearing that they would be
punished for their previous wrongdoing, the brothers were surprised
to find that Joseph treated them kindly and invited them to his house
for a meal. Joseph sustained them. Whether they knew it or not, God
brought about this act of restoration. Regardless of Joseph's journey,
God's word through Joseph's dream and His promises were still
true. Joseph's dream was fulfilled a second time when his brothers
prostrated themselves before him, and from his second seat, Joseph
provided for his brothers lavishly.

Joseph felt no need for retaliation, and I think a test of our power and position occurs when the people who disregarded our dreams, passed us along the way, or failed to create opportunities for us end up seated on the other side of our table. By not retaliating, you literally allow the moment to bring about restoration and healing in your relationships. Don't burn any bridges. From your seat, be trustworthy because God will always test you in positions of power to see how you manage or how you handle power when you're on the other side.

Don't burn the bridges God has built.

This was a real epiphany for Joseph: remembering the dream, recognizing his brothers, and then going for reconciliation instead of retaliation—twice! Though they still don't recognize who he is, he's still building a relationship and trying to see if they've had a change of heart by how he favors Benjamin and gives Benjamin more. How we in power—regardless of the location of our seat—treat people in their moments of weakness after they have intentionally exploited our weakness reveals our comfort level in the seat God has placed us in.

You develop a sensitivity for other people when God allows you to come from the bottom of a pit to the top—when He puts into your hands someone who has crushed you in theirs. It's important that you handle people in the way that you would want them to handle you, even if they didn't handle you in that way. It's a true test of character and a true test of power.

> **Handle others the way you wish they had handled you.**

It's also worth mentioning that before Jacob relented and allowed his older sons to take Benjamin back to Egypt, Judah had to intervene and make a special appeal to his father:

> *"Send the boy along with me . . . . I myself will guarantee his safety; you can hold me personally responsible for him. If I do not bring him back to you and set him here before you, I will bear the blame before you all my life."* —Genesis 43:9

Judah's descendants would take their seat as the progenitors of Christ, and Joseph's second-in-command seat made that possible. This is more evidence that one person's dream can be manifest in the context of another's. Nothing is wasted in God's economy. Yes, God *could* have gone about this differently and without Joseph having suffered what he did. But God didn't. At God's table, every seat is equally valuable, and no seat should be deemed an indicator of God's favor of one person over another. All dreams are coming to fruition through cooperation with others—in conjunction with others. That mutual sense of accomplishment and satisfaction is the sweet spot.

> **That mutual sense of satisfaction is the sweet spot!**

Too often, leaders are so focused on their own dream that everyone else's becomes subservient to theirs, but Joseph's dream could only be fulfilled as he interpreted Pharaoh's. That was the sweet spot. I reached my own sweet spot when I moved back to Chicago and started working with New Life. Pastor Hannah was already doing what I believed needed to be done. I could have pridefully insisted on doing it myself, or I could accept the seat New Life offered me. Both of our dreams would be realized for the glory of God and His kingdom. How are you actively joining your dreams with others and sharing the sweet spot with them at the table?

If you need a check and balance to make sure you're in the sweet spot, remember to S.E.R.V.E the seat. It's what we're all called to do.

SERVE
See the Future
Engage & Equip others
Reinvent continuously
Value results & relationships
Embody the values

This was what Joseph did for Pharaoh and all of Egypt. As a result, he got to see his dreams come full circle too.

CHAPTER 9

STANDING UP TO YOUR TEST

GENESIS 44

If Joseph's story were unfolding on the big screen, by now, we would have witnessed Joseph—from the pit to the palace—plotting his brothers' demise. His brothers wouldn't have had to find him, inadvertently or otherwise. From the first moment he was in a position to call the shots, he would have put plans into motion not only to realize his dreams but also to make sure his brothers realized them too. And after a night of wining and dining his adversaries, when their defenses were down, we would expect Joseph to move in for the kill.

Every seat at the table exerts influence.

What happened in Genesis 44 was classic Hollywood, but the outcome was not. Joseph had a plan, and the leadership character that God had spent the previous decades developing in him was about to spill over to those around him. I mentioned at the beginning of this book that our leadership is never just about us. I believe that everyone is a leader. Every seat at the table exerts influence—sometimes good, sometimes bad—based on a person's strengths and weaknesses.

As Joseph's brothers set off for home, he put the last phase of his plan—one that would expose the strengths and weakness of all involved—in motion. It would test his brothers' mettle. It would also reveal their capacity to repent and Joseph's to show mercy.

> Now Joseph gave these instructions to the steward of his house: "Fill the men's sacks with as much food as they can carry, and put each man's silver in the mouth of his sack. Then put my cup, the silver one, in the mouth of the youngest one's sack, along with the silver for his grain." And he did as Joseph said.
>
> As morning dawned, the men were sent on their way with their donkeys. They had not gone far from the city when Joseph said to his steward, "Go after those men at once, and when you catch up with them, say to them, 'Why have you repaid good with evil? Isn't this the cup my master drinks from and also uses for divination? This is a wicked thing you have done.'"

When he caught up with them, he repeated these words to them. But they said to him, "Why does my lord say such things? . . . If any of your servants is found to have it, he will die; and the rest of us will become my lord's slaves."

"Very well, then," he said, "let it be as you say. Whoever is found to have it will become my slave; the rest of you will be free from blame."

Each of them quickly lowered his sack to the ground and opened it. Then the steward proceeded to search, beginning with the oldest and ending with the youngest. And the cup was found in Benjamin's sack. At this, they tore their clothes. Then they all loaded their donkeys and returned to the city.

Joseph was still in the house when Judah and his brothers came in, and they threw themselves to the ground before him . . . .

"What can we say to my lord?" Judah replied. "What can we say? How can we prove our innocence? God has uncovered your servants' guilt. We are now my lord's slaves—we ourselves and the one who was found to have the cup."

But Joseph said, "Far be it from me to do such a thing! Only the man who was found to have the cup will become my slave. The rest of you, go back to your father in peace."

Then Judah went up to him and said: "Pardon your servant, my lord, let me speak a word to my lord. Do not be angry with your servant, though you are equal to Pharaoh himself . . . ."
—Genesis 44:1–6 and 10–18

Two storylines run concurrently through this chapter. In previous chapters, we followed Joseph's development from an impetuous youth, sitting in the seat of favor in his father's household and sharing his dreams without much concern for how they would impact others to operating as Pharaoh's second-in-command, sharing his ability to interpret dreams to make the greatest impact for good at home and abroad. During this time, Joseph's brothers had undergone the maturation process as well. Imagine the disaster if they had not humbled themselves. We must be experts at extending forgiveness.

> **We must be experts at extending forgiveness.**

For Joseph's brothers, if the nightmare of growing up in a household plagued by favoritism and rivalry, living in a land devastated by famine and beholden to a foreign power for survival, and bearing a decades-long burden of secrecy and shame were not enough, they were facing their ultimate horror. They were going to lose Benjamin and cause what was left of their father to die of heartbreak. And their honor was at stake.

Notice how the men responded when Joseph's steward approached them, accusing them of having stolen from his master: "If any of your servants is found to have [your master's cup], he will die; and the rest of us will become my lord's slaves" (Genesis 44:9). They were confident that they were innocent. While the brothers had plotted against and argued with each other in the past, they were on the same page this time. They had brought the silver used to pay for the first installment of food back with them to Egypt in case there had been some mistake when it was placed in their bags. Their belief in their innocence was furthered by the consequences they propose if the steward found Joseph's cup in their possession. The thief would die, and the rest would become slaves.

Their attitude toward their father's favorites had changed too. If they viewed Benjamin the way they viewed Joseph, they would have been glad to be rid of him. When they had decided what to do with Joseph back in Genesis 37, they had opted to do more than just remove him from the family. They had capitalized on the situation and actually benefitted by selling him to an Ishmaelite caravan. And this time they wouldn't have to blame Jacob's favorite's disappearance on a wild animal as they had when they took Joseph's bloodied coat to their father. They could send word to their father that Benjamin deserved his punishment, and it was Benjamin's fault Jacob had lost *all* of his sons!

However, we can tell from Judah's reply that much has changed. When pleading with Joseph about how they could prove their innocence, he made the following statement: "God has uncovered your servants' guilt." He wasn't referring to the guilt of theft. They were innocent. But the guilt of what they'd done to Joseph, in their minds, was being rightfully punished through this situation. This is a markedly different response to what they'd done the first time. When you find yourself in a situation that requires you to backtrack or eat your words or rethink your attitude, what do you do?

Further showing how they'd changed, Judah went into detail regarding his last conversation with Jacob before the trip in his explanation:

» He quoted his father: "You know that my wife bore me two sons. One of them went away from me, and I said, 'He has surely been torn to pieces. And I have not seen him since. If you take this one from me too and harm comes to him, you will bring my gray head down to the grave in misery" (verses 27-29).

» He acknowledged that Jacob's life was "bound up in the boy's life" and that he couldn't bear to bring such sorrow to his father (verses 30-31).

» He reiterated his vow to bear the blame if for whatever reason Benjamin was not to make it back to Jacob safely (verse 32).

» He offered himself—in place of Benjamin—as Joseph's slave (verse 33).

Therefore, Joseph's testing of his brothers revealed their change of heart toward a favored brother and a father whose heart was still not shared equally among them. It allowed Judah to step into his position of leadership as a son willing to be taken into slavery himself to keep that relationship intact—unlike severing it in Joseph's case. And it brought Joseph's dream to the forefront again when his brothers bowed to him a third time.

It's funny how life works sometimes. In this shocking turn of events, Joseph's brothers ended up back in his life, looking for help. Joseph's embracing the seat God had provided for him allowed him to

DR. JERMONE T. GLENN

show mercy. It flowed over into his brothers' lives, and that is evident in Judah's response after Joseph told them, "Only the man who was found to have the cup will become my slave. The rest of you, go back to your father in peace." There would be no peace if each hadn't men stood up to the test and taken their seat at the table.

> **People who called me crazy now called for consultations.**

I found the same thing to be true. The same people who called me crazy for streaming church now came to me for consultations on streaming. By the time of the COVID-19 pandemic, I had been implementing modern technology to broadcast the message of God's kingdom for close to fifteen years. For over a decade, our church had been breaking away from the more traditional ways of worship. In addition to hardback Bibles, I encouraged my people to use their phones and tablets. In addition to singing using hymnals, we had started projecting lyrics to popular worship songs on-screen. My contemporaries accused me of entertaining because we dimmed the lights and utilized more dramatic stage techniques with smoke and lighting to get people's attention.

In our efforts to get the gospel out beyond the four walls of our building, we encouraged our congregation to text and tweet and post to their Facebook pages—during the message. We had people at home watching our services online and calling in for prayer. Other pastors accused me of not valuing the in-person church experience and creating a false sense of community by allowing those who were not present in body to be present in heart and mind. Allegedly, I was distracting them from the church's true purpose, but I had known already that the main thing was to advance God's kingdom—not advance the church. The kingdom was the end. The church was the means to get there.

Everything at the beginning was innovative: illustrated messages and movie clips to communicate the gospel, modern stories to illustrate biblical truth, and popular culture references to make connections to people's lives. People wondered and often asked, "What are you doing here?" "What kind of church is this?" And, our church was called The Revolution. It was designed to be counter-cultural (church culture, that is). We deliberately integrated new methods to communicate an age-old message. We set precedents for bringing Christ to culture. After all, that's what Jesus did. He used parables and references that the people of his time understood and brought the kingdom of God face-to-face with culture. Jesus went where others wouldn't so he could do what others couldn't. We modeled our ministry to do the same.

> **Jesus went where others wouldn't so he could do what others couldn't.**

Then, when the pandemic hit, and people were forbidden to leave their homes and gather in churches, some leaders were stuck. They weren't ready. Many other churches around the US had implemented a multicampus model with numerous congregations gathering in different locations, worshiping together and hearing a single message preached on-screen. They had utilized wireless technology and various social media platforms, but it just wasn't common outside of my circle in my tradition.

I found myself in the exact same position as Joseph. The world was experiencing a spiritual-gathering famine. The majority of people, unable to congregate in person, were scared, isolated, and starving. And all those other ministers who thought I was too progressive came to me asking for advice. We lived in the future and knew we were both a prototype and a Paradigm so we were excited to share what we perfected from many years of mistakes. I had no idea so many leaders were technologically challenged. When that happened, I was tested. I, too, could have said, "I told you so!" But that is not what happened.

My gift of communication and teaching came in handy again. I wrote a tech e-book called *Tech Is Next*, which contained links to products, websites, and other resources and gave it away for free, just so other pastors knew what hardware and software they needed in order to continue to feed their congregations. Because of how the Lord gifted me, and because of the seats He had provided for me as I endeavored to fulfill my vision for my life, I had experience that other people needed—similar to Joseph interpreting Pharoah's dream, organizing the famine relief, and implementing the program. And, because I wanted to guard my heart and embrace my seat, I shared it.

So, the people who once turned on you will be back around, and the ultimate test of your leadership will be your ability to show mercy. Leadership is about serving. If God gives you a position of authority or a position in leadership, it's not about being served; it is about following Jesus's *modus operandi*. It's about the responsibility of empowering people who were once in your seat or your position and removing barriers and creating opportunities for them to use their gifts and talents and find their place of self-expression.

God put Joseph in a position to save his family. And it was painful for everyone involved because God removed him from his family's dynamic—first in a very negative way but also in a way that brought his vision of himself in the future to fruition. If you remember, in chapter 2 of this book and Genesis 37:8, after telling his brothers his dream, they responded: "Do you intend to reign over us? Will you actually rule us?" His dream and his retelling of it caused them to hate him all the more. If they had known that Joseph's being in power would not only rescue his family and bring them to a safe place but also save the entire region, their response might have been different. But no one but God knows the future.

So, I believe that all leadership is about putting you in a place to serve and not be served—to use your wisdom, skills, gifts, and talents to empower and help other people. And I do think that his brothers, once they realized he wasn't going to take revenge on them, found comfort at that moment—that space of his revelation and his place of authority. It was not what they expected because this position of power protected and preserved them as well as their father. This reigning and ruling was not a bad thing.

> **Leadership puts you in a place to serve—not be served.**

I see my personal responsibility or space in leadership is definitely not about myself but about others. Whom can I serve? Where can I serve, and how can I help other people find their ability to serve? How can I help other people discover and find their purpose and be empowered to manifest that?

Joseph's leadership was definitely not about being himself, and even though his brothers misinterpreted it that way, nothing Joseph did from the moment he got into power was about himself. Everything was about interpreting someone else's dream and applying the wisdom from that interpretation to create, implement, and sustain a system of economic stability, protection, and prosperity in a moment of crisis or a pandemic.

In what ways does your purpose empower others to find theirs and manifest it to expand the kingdom?

CHAPTER 10

SOLIDIFYING YOUR IDENTITY
GENESIS 45

In Chapter 8: "Sitting Together," we read about Joseph's response when he saw his brother Benjamin. Genesis 43:29 says that Joseph blessed him: "God be gracious to you, my son." Then, because Joseph was about to be overcome by his emotions, he hurried from the room, so he could weep in private. After witnessing Judah's heartfelt plea, however, he could control himself no longer. He was not getting any joy or satisfaction out of their plight; he was ready to be known by his brothers for who he truly was.

Genesis 45 describes what happened next:

Then Joseph could no longer control himself before all his atten- dants, and he cried out, "Have everyone leave my presence!" So there was no one with Joseph when he made himself known to his brothers. And he wept so loudly that the Egyptians heard him, and Pharaoh's household heard about it.

Joseph said to his brothers, "I am Joseph! Is my father still living?" But his brothers were not able to answer him, because they were terrified at his presence.

Then Joseph said to his brothers, "Come close to me." When they had done so, he said, "I am your brother Joseph, the one you sold into Egypt! And now, do not be distressed and do not be angry with yourselves for selling me here, because it was to save lives that God sent me ahead of you. For two years now there has been famine in the land, and for the next five years there will be no plowing and reaping. But God sent me ahead of you to preserve for you a remnant on earth and to save your lives by a great deliverance. [a]

"So then, it was not you who sent me here, but God. He made me father to Pharaoh, lord of his entire household and ruler of all Egypt. Now hurry back to my father and say to him, 'This is what your son Joseph says: God has made me lord of all Egypt. Come down to me; don't delay. You shall live in the region of Goshen and be near me—you, your children and grandchildren, your flocks and herds, and all you have. I will provide for you there, because five years of famine are still to come. Otherwise you and your household and all who belong to you will become destitute.'

"You can see for yourselves, and so can my brother Benjamin, that it is really I who am speaking to you. Tell my father about

all the honor accorded me in Egypt and about everything you have seen. And bring my father down here quickly."

Then he threw his arms around his brother Benjamin and wept, and Benjamin embraced him, weeping. And he kissed all his brothers and wept over them. Afterward his brothers talked with him. —Genesis 45:1-15

People often talk about their destiny—what they were made for. Their identity, though, usually just comes from how they see themselves or what they do for a job. I believe that a person's identity is a bigger part of their destiny because your identity is as connected to your future as the other parts of your life that lead to your destiny. Your purpose is why you were born. Your vision or your dream is a preview of your purpose—how you are going to get there. And, the various seats that you sit in as you lead in your sphere of influence showcase what you can do. In the words of Dr. Myles Monroe: "Leadership is the capacity to influence others through inspiration motivated by passion, generated by vision, produced by a conviction, ignited by a purpose."[6]

Identities don't change. They change other things.

---

6   Myles Munroe, *The Power of Character in Leadership: How Values, Morals, Ethics, and Principles Affect Leaders* (New Kensington, PA: Whitaker House, 2014) 34.

Identity is hidden in destiny, and your life is meant to reveal its mystery through your identity because identity remains the same in various conditions or circumstances. It doesn't change. It changes other things. Ultimately, our identities are found in our relationship with Christ. We are who He says we are, and He reveals that as we look at our past, take our position in the seat God has provided for our present, and use them to become what He has planned for our future as He brings us closer to our destiny. What we become—in many ways—is more important than what we do. That's why we can't base our identity on our occupation, position in our family, GPA, or role that we fill. Those things are only avenues for us to reveal our identity.

Every label creates a limit, but when we focus on who we are instead of what we do or how other people see us, we can still be ourselves—no matter where we are. I was still Jermone Glenn when I was a senior pastor. I am still Jermone Glenn as an executive pastor. I am Jermone Glenn, whether I am a pastor, a husband, a father, a son, a brother, or a friend. It's like I said in chapter 1: I am. Therefore, I do.

I am. Therefore, I do.

When it was time, Joseph revealed his identity to his brothers: "I AM JOSEPH!" He was secure in who he was because he had been walking in purpose, vision, and leadership the whole time.

He had endured heart- and spirit-breaking circumstances. His role had changed—he had sat in many seats—during his lifetime (and he was only in his thirties when this part of his story took place!), yet his identity hadn't changed. He had sat in the favored-son seat, the hated-brother seat, the slave seat, the wrongly accused seat, the problem-solver seat, and the second-in-command seat. Each was an integral part of fulfilling his destiny. He knew—and had known all along—exactly who he was. Labels limit. Identities liberate.

> ## Labels limit. Identities liberate.

One of the reasons Joseph's brothers didn't recognize him is because they were burdened by their memories of the past. They had treated him abominably, and in their minds, he was still that teenager they had sold into slavery. Every time they thought of him, they probably thought either of his boasting about his dream of them bowing down to him or their selling him into slavery. Both of those thoughts paralyzed them. As a matter of fact, the first time Joseph told them who he was, they were "terrified in his presence," according to Genesis 45. They had not expected to see him ever again. They had no frame of reference for the Joseph they saw in this position—this place. He had to repeat himself to get their attention and snap them back to the present.

Another reason they didn't recognize him was because they had not acknowledged his dream. They heard the dream but didn't believe the dream; they had scoffed at it, so when they saw him in the manifestation of the dream, he did not look the same to them. It's possible that they hadn't even made the connection that their bowing on those previous occasions had validated Joseph's dream. Joseph's identity was hidden from them—both in Canaan and in Egypt, until that moment. It was now time for them to know him, and Joseph told them who he was and how God had orchestrated His plan. It's almost like Joseph could have asked them at the beginning: "Will you know me . . . can you recognize me . . . in my shall be?" They hadn't recognized him, and they were terrified on all fronts.

Everything that had happened in Joseph's life was preparing him for a future that didn't exist yet. God knew Joseph's true identity—as a young man and the second-in-command. Many people would put plans into action when it came to what Joseph experienced, but at the same time, Joseph's response would be creating his future. God put Joseph in positions that would bring about His plan—which was to save many lives—and Joseph made that clear in verse five when told his brothers not to be angry with themselves. God had sent Joseph before them. God had a problem that needed solving. He had made provision for Joseph to solve it. His brothers needed to see his purpose at the moment—in that seat.

It's not always others, though, who limit us with labels. Sometimes we restrain ourselves. I've known leaders who refused to relinquish their seats because they valued their position more than their purpose. They actually impeded their personal and professional growth because they couldn't separate the two. God had placed them in the seat they occupied; make no mistake about that. But it was for a time and a purpose. God hadn't wasted their skills. He had used them to further His kingdom, but they were stuck in their role—they mistook it for their identity—and for a time, they impeded their own progress and God's purpose for them. Joseph's heart was in the right place, and by serving his seat as a ruler and a brother, he would fulfill his purpose.

To further analyze where Joseph's heart was, he drew his brothers to him. They would be able to see him up close and hear his voice because he started talking to them in their own language. He was not acting as a stranger would. He did not keep his second-in-command persona on like a shield. Instead, he fully revealed himself to them and exposed his heart by asking about their father. Upon hearing that he was alive, Joseph instructed them to go get him and bring him and all their families back to Egypt. If Joseph had lost himself in the pursuit of his dream, he wouldn't have been in the seat that he needed to be in to accomplish his dream—God's dream for him.

Finally, when it comes to identity, God exposes you to who needs to know you. When Joseph first told his brothers about his dreams, they didn't need to know. Joseph's vision served no purpose for them, other than to drive them to disgust and to plot against him. However, at this point, while it had already been painful—they'd had to make several trips to Egypt simply to feed their families—they were in a position to see Joseph and them living in Joseph's vision. They needed their brother and his vision because both would serve them.

Joseph's vision would serve their father too:

So they went up out of Egypt and came to their father Jacob in the land of Canaan. They told him, "Joseph is still alive! In fact, he is ruler of all Egypt." Jacob was stunned; he did not believe them. But when they told him everything Joseph had said to them, and when he saw the carts Joseph had sent to carry him back, the spirit of their father Jacob revived. And Israel said, "I'm convinced! My son Joseph is still alive. I will go and see him before I die." —Genesis 45:25-28

Joseph revealed his true identity to his brothers. He forgave them for their past wrongdoings and invited them to bring their families to Egypt to live in safety during the remainder of the famine, so Jacob and his family traveled to Egypt to live with Joseph.

There is much to be said about destiny—where we want to go, who we want to become, and what we want to do, but little to be said about identity—who we are and what we're made of. Destiny is settled in identity, and both work to further the kingdom. All those years apart, God was working on and through Joseph as well as his brothers and father. Each of us also must search our hearts during our lives to answer questions about our identity, heritage, purpose, and potential. And like Joseph, we only fulfill our purpose and manifest our destiny when we participate in the transformational life and well-being of our communities. How well are you doing that?

Destiny is settled in identity.

CHAPTER 11

SAFEGUARDING YOUR STRENGTHS

GENESIS 47

If Joseph's story had ended with his revealing his identity to his brothers, forgiving them for the heartbreak they had caused him and his father, mother, and younger brother, and inviting his father and the rest of the family to live out the rest of the famine in Egypt, it would have been a glorious finale. Joseph's dream had come true, he was vindicated by his brothers' obvious remorse, and he'd become a hero to millions of people. But God was not done yet. He had more promises to keep, more dreams to bring to fruition, and more visions to give. The next would be to Jacob.

> **God had more promises to keep, more dreams to bring to fruition, and more visions to give.**

Genesis 46 describes what happened after Jacob packed up his household and headed to Egypt:

So Israel set out with all that was his, and when he reached Beersheba, he offered sacrifices to the God of his father Isaac.

And God spoke to Israel in a vision at night and said, "Jacob! Jacob!"

"Here I am," he replied.

"I am God, the God of your father," he said. "Do not be afraid to go down to Egypt, for I will make you into a great nation there. I will go down to Egypt with you, and I will surely bring you back again. And Joseph's own hand will close your eyes."

Then Jacob left Beersheba, and Israel's sons took their father Jacob and their children and their wives in the carts that Pharaoh had sent to transport him. So Jacob and all his offspring went to Egypt, taking with them their livestock and the possessions they had acquired in Canaan. Jacob brought with him to Egypt his sons and grandsons and his daughters and granddaughters—all his offspring . . . .

Now Jacob sent Judah ahead of him to Joseph to get directions to Goshen. When they arrived in the region of Goshen, Joseph had his chariot made ready and went to Goshen to meet his father Israel. As soon as Joseph appeared before him, he threw his arms around his father and wept for a long time.

Israel said to Joseph, "Now I am ready to die, since I have seen for myself that you are still alive."

Then Joseph said to his brothers and to his father's household, "I will go up and speak to Pharaoh and will say to him, 'My brothers and my father's household, who were living in the land of Canaan, have come to me. The men are shepherds; they tend livestock, and they have brought along their flocks and herds and everything they own.' When Pharaoh calls you in and asks, 'What is your occupation?' you should answer, 'Your servants have tended livestock from our boyhood on, just as our fathers did.' Then you will be allowed to settle in the region of Goshen, for all shepherds are detestable to the Egyptians."
—Genesis 47:1-7 and 28-33

God spoke to Jacob in a vision—similar to the way He had spoken to Jacob's grandfather Abraham. In Abraham's vision in Genesis 15, God promised him and his barren wife Sarah an entire nation of descendants that would fill an abundant land as far as his eyes could see. It would not come easily to them, though:

Then the Lord said to him, "Know for certain that for four hundred years your descendants will be strangers in a country not their own and that they will be enslaved and mistreated there. But I will punish the nation they serve as slaves, and afterward they will come out with great possessions. You, however, will

go to your ancestors in peace and be buried at a good old age.
—*Genesis 15:13–15*

In Genesis 47, Jacob found himself leaving that land. Perhaps Jacob felt like he was losing one dream to embrace another. He would give up his inheritance—Canaan, a land in which he had been a foreigner but he now possessed—for the sake of seeing his son, whom he'd feared was dead and providing for the longevity of his family line. Perhaps he was wondering if *his* children would be the ones who became enslaved before returning to their land. Whatever he was experiencing, God reassured Jacob that his descendants would become a great nation—even in Egypt. God would *go with* them and then bring them back home again.

When they arrived, Joseph was waiting to meet them. Jacob had sent Judah ahead of the large group, so he could meet with Joseph and direct them to where they would settle. We know already that Egyptians did not eat with Israelites. When the brothers ate at Joseph's palace, they were separated from him. Joseph provided a safe separation for his family in their new land too. He arranged with Pharaoh to settle them in the land of Goshen.

The word Goshen comes from the Hebrew word *gushan* which means "drawing out" or "separation."[7] The land of Goshen was right on the border between Canaan and Egypt. According to *Layman's Bible Commentary*, "Goshen had some of the best pastureland in all of Egypt. It would be a place to keep the Hebrews isolated and insulated

---

7   Harold Williams, "What Is the Spiritual Meaning of Goshen?" *SpiritualDesk*, 23 Apr. 2023, spiritualdesk.com/what-is-the-spiritual-meaning-of-goshen/.

from the culture and religion of Egypt."[8] In this place, God showed His divine providence once again. Providence comes from the Latin word *providentia* which essentially means foresight or making provision beforehand. We can see from His words to Abraham that God knew what would happen. Connecting that belief with Joseph's belief that God orchestrated everything shows how extraordinary Joseph really was too.

Joseph internalized Jacob's affirmation.

Jacob knew Joseph was special; he was unique. Jacob gave Joseph that coat of many colors we hear about when we're children (see Genesis 37) to distinguish him from his brothers. Maybe that was why Joseph could believe the dream that his brothers would bow to him. He had internalized that affirming picture of himself. He could see himself the way his father saw him and embrace it. Now, he would use the favor that Pharoah showed him to provide a safe haven for his father in a time of famine and fear. To imagine that Pharaoh so valued Joseph that he provided carts, so his family could move all their possessions. That's like your boss paying for a moving truck to relocate your distant relatives to be closer to you! Most of us are lucky if our bosses pay to move *us*!

---

8   KD Manes, "Why Did Joseph Want His Family to Settle in Goshen?" *Kdmanestreet*, 26 Aug. 2016, kdmanestreet.com/tag/why-did-joseph-want-his-family-to-settle-in-goshen/.

Finally, the moment that Jacob and Joseph had been waiting for since finding out that each other was still alive came. All the years of living and grieving, broken and tormented, traumatized by losing each other probably melted away. The Bible only mentions Joseph throwing his arms around Jacob and sobbing for a long time. However, we all know it was mutual. Jacob felt like everything he had ever hoped for—and much that he hadn't dared hope for—had come to pass. At that moment—face to face with his long-lost son—he beheld Joseph with his own eyes. He could die happy, knowing Joseph was alive and thriving.

What Jacob had always believed for and hoped for was confirmed. He recognized the power of his son's position. And only God could have put his son in the seat he was serving in: a place of power and authority, decision-making, dreaming, the dream-interpreting. What a moment for Jacob! What a moment for Joseph to be able to show his father that what he thought of his son, what he spoke over him, how he marked him, and how he acknowledged him was spot-on.

When I was a young boy, I had some unique qualities too. Some were easy to appreciate. Others weren't. I frequently got in trouble at school for talking. I was constantly looking toward the future. As a matter of fact, one day, early on, my dad told me he thought I was going to grow up to be an astronaut. It took me over ten years to figure out that he wasn't talking about an *actual* astronaut! He meant that he saw me doing things differently than other people; I was a forerunner, a trailblazer. I had no fear of uncharted territory. And my father validated that in me and expressed pride in my gifts.

As far as that gift for talking that I constantly got in trouble with my teachers for? What can I say? I was a natural communicator! What was a weakness at that point in time has become a great strength for me. That thread runs through all of our lives. When the time is right because God is ready for us to use traits that made us precocious when we were younger—if they've been stewarded well—they will serve others and further God's kingdom.

> ## Jacob could have done a better job safeguarding Joseph's strengths.

Jacob could have done a better job of that with Joseph. He could have safeguarded Joseph's vision, his dreams. He could have encouraged and affirmed him without drawing so much attention to him that Joseph's brothers hated their father's favorite. Instead, his brothers turned Joseph's greatest strength against him. And what about if we're the leaders calling out gifts and fostering them in others?

In our leadership roles—from the perspectives of our seats—how do we identify gifts in those we lead? What's unique or special about those whom God has entrusted to you? How do you nurture, protect, preserve, and cultivate those qualities in people, so they also affirm and understand their assignments? How do parents do that for their children, teachers for their students, and mentors for their mentees?

If we are in Joseph's position, how do we appreciate and celebrate all the people—the mentors, fathers, mothers, teachers, pastors—who contributed to our calling and our growth. How do we recognize those who helped us develop skills, sort out our lives, and identify in a sense what's unique or what's special about us? Find a way to honor them or reward them. Affirm their role with you, and allow them to take their seats right with you at the table.

I wrote a whole book recently called *Mentors*. In it, I honored all of my teachers and the lessons I learned from them. I shared anecdotes about their investments in me and explained how when I'm in any position or any room, I'm standing on their shoulders. I'm representing them. My presence is a result of their influence in my life. They saw something in me—whether I was in the janitor's seat or the executive's seat—and called it out. We must never underestimate the power of embracing and doing right by the people who did right by us. I see that principle in the relationship between Joseph's father and Joseph's master. Pharaoh extended his appreciation of Joseph to Jacob. Jacob was, after all, the man who brought Joseph into the world and raised him to be the man he became—the man who saved Pharaoh's entire kingdom from certain disaster.

> **Never underestimate the power of doing right by the people who did right by you.**

We know already that Pharaoh authorized Joseph to give his father and brothers the land of Goshen, but he didn't stop there. With Joseph's brothers' skill with animals, Pharaoh also offered them jobs taking care of his flocks and herds. Egyptians were mostly farmers, depending on the Nile River due to its rich soil caused by annual flooding. It was in Pharaoh's best interest to have real herdsmen in charge of his animals. Undoubtedly, Pharaoh figured his animals would thrive under their care. The blessing would be mutual. Simply by residing in Egypt in close proximity to Joseph and the stored provisions, they would be secure. Pharaoh's offer of work, though, also provided an opportunity for them to actually support themselves. They would not be living off of Joseph's (and Egypt's) generosity.

Of all the questions Pharaoh could ask Jacob when he met him, he asked him how old he was. It's possible Jacob looked older than he was since he answered in Genesis 47:9 (BSB) with the following:

> "My travels have lasted 130 years," Jacob replied. "My years have been few and hard, and they have not matched the years of the travels of my fathers."

It's not hard to imagine that Jacob was careworn. Since he was in the womb, he'd been struggling against his brother. Then, he struggled against his uncle. Surely, he struggled against his sons since it was obvious that he played favorites. A years-long famine would have worn him down even more. Yet seeing Joseph again would have given him a new lease on life. Therefore, Jacob blessed Pharaoh and spent the rest of his life—seventeen years—cared for by Joseph in a land where his family "acquired property . . . and became fruitful and increased greatly in number" (Genesis 47:27, BSB).

What do we do when we're tired or jaded? When we feel like our dreams have been mismanaged by ourselves and others? We keep living, problem-solving, and capitalizing on our strengths. When you look at your path and the seat that you're in, and it looks different than what you'd planned . . . look for the familiar! The Lord's got this, and He's just fulfilling the dream through a different arena. Don't kill the dream. Cultivate it, and make a space for it.

Don't kill the dream. Cultivate it.

Pharaoh—like Jacob—saw the promise in Joseph. The gift that Jacob saw in Joseph came to fruition with Pharaoh. Pharaoh trusted Joseph to take the ball of the famine and run with it. We also get the best out of leaders when they are empowered to do their jobs using their unique strengths in the way they see fit to use them. How are you allowing yourself and those you lead to fully utilize the gifts that God has given each of you for His kingdom purposes?

DR. JERMONE T. GLENN

CHAPTER 12

SEEKING RECONCILIATION

GENESIS 49 AND 50

Before Jacob's death, he called his sons together, so he could "bless" them. He spoke poignantly regarding each's strengths and weaknesses and prophesied about their descendants based on what he, as their father, saw in them. His words about Joseph indicate that, by now, he knew what had transpired between him and his brothers. He also saw God's hand at work:

> "Joseph is a fruitful bough,
> a fruitful bough by a spring;
> his branches run over the wall.
> The archers bitterly attacked him,
> shot at him, and harassed him severely,
> yet his bow remained unmoved;

> *his arms were made agile*
> *by the hands of the Mighty One of Jacob . . . .*
> *The blessings of your father*
> *are mighty beyond the blessings of my parents,*
> *up to the bounties of the everlasting hills.*
> *May they be on the head of Joseph,*
> *and on the brow of him who was set apart from his brothers."*
> *—Genesis 49:22–24 and 26 (ESV)*

The picture of Joseph is that of a lush vine, nourished by freshwater, that grows out into all directions, sharing its fruit and its shade. Considering that Joseph singlehandedly saved the nations during the years of famine, that was an apt description. He portrayed Joseph's brothers as archers who "bitterly attacked him," yet God was on his side and sustained his strength. Jacob finished by recounting his blessings as Joseph's father and wishing them to be on his son "who was set apart from his brothers." After seventeen years of living in close proximity to his father, Joseph promised that Jacob's bones would be buried in Canaan, and Jacob drew his last breath. The remarkable bond and affection between son and father is evidenced by Genesis 50:1 (NLT): "Joseph threw himself on his father and wept over him and kissed him."

Joseph kept his promise. He directed his physicians to embalm his father so that the body could be transported from Egypt to Canaan. Then, with his household, his brothers, and numerous Egyptian representatives, Joseph grieved his father to the point that the Canaanite inhabitants who saw the procession remarked upon it.

Would Joseph use his power for payback?

Now that their father was gone, would Joseph use his power for payback? Joseph's brothers would test his position of leadership one more time:

> When Joseph's brothers saw that their father was dead, they said, "What if Joseph holds a grudge against us and pays us back for all the wrongs we did to him?" So they sent word to Joseph, saying, "Your father left these instructions before he died: 'This is what you are to say to Joseph: I ask you to forgive your brothers the sins and the wrongs they committed in treating you so badly.' Now please forgive the sins of the servants of the God of your father." When their message came to him, Joseph wept.
>
> His brothers then came and threw themselves down before him. "We are your slaves," they said.
>
> But Joseph said to them, "Don't be afraid. Am I in the place of God? You intended to harm me, but God intended it for good to accomplish what is now being done, the saving of many lives. So then, don't be afraid. I will provide for you and your children." And he reassured them and spoke kindly to them. — Genesis 50:15-21

Maybe it was human nature that Joseph's brothers were still suspicious of him. They didn't recognize his dream or appreciate his potential when they were younger. He had attempted to convince them seventeen years earlier that although they had sold him into slavery, God had ultimately sent him ahead of them to Egypt in order that they and many others would be preserved during the famine. He had embraced them, wept with them, told them not to be distressed or angry with themselves, and provided for them, but their guilt still gripped them. In their minds, this would be the perfect time for Joseph to exact his revenge.

Therefore, they sent a messenger ahead of them to give a bogus request on behalf of their father. They knew that it would be just for Joseph to retaliate. If he had previously held back because he didn't want to cause his father any more pain, his continued position of prestige in Egypt would allow him to seek retribution at this time. However, Joseph—true to form—wept. The Bible doesn't say why. Perhaps, it was just in *his* nature. Maybe it was because they humbled themselves and fell to their faces again, promising to be his servant. Possibly it was because even after all those years, they still didn't know him or trust his character.

Regardless, Joseph—again—submitted to the seat that God had put him in: favored son, dreamer, slave, household steward, dream interpreter, kingdom administrator, family benefactor, promise keeper, and now . . . forgiving brother. Can you pass the test? Are you able to forgive and forget like nothing ever happened? Joseph could've condemned his brothers forever. If he did, he would have upended the future. What is hanging on your ability to forgive?

Our natural tendency is to right wrongs—especially wrongs done to us. We have to intentionally posture ourselves to give mercy to others, even if we deem them undeserving. Being in leadership means you take on a lot. You get wounded by wounded people all the time. You get mishandled, even by those you once served alongside.

If leading from the second seat can show you anything, it is that there is much miscommunication that causes pain for leaders and followers. You see how easily things can be twisted and turned until minuscule problems become major issues. Being a minister of mercy means you have the ability to help ease the pains of leaders and followers.

You know what it's like, but you also see the problem from your unique perspective in the second seat. That's why you're called to sit in it. However, you can't reign with contention in your heart. That's a setup. You have to heal, so you can handle your role.

> **You can't reign with contention in your heart.**

If Joseph had taken revenge on his brothers, he would've become like Potiphar and all those who condemned him. But when he stepped in as a restorative person, he was modeling Christ.

As a leader serving other leaders, you get to prove the power of partnership. Purpose needs partners. You get to show how two can truly put ten thousand to flight. But what happens when you and the leader you serve bump heads? Do you walk away because this isn't your dream anyway? No! That's not a possibility, and if it is in your mind, that means you haven't taken your seat in the correct place. You must be an expert on forgiveness.

> **We must be experts on forgiveness.**

Joseph ultimately forgave. We can too. Take a moment to think of areas where you may need to forgive.

After the experience I described in chapter 4 when Bishop Abney changed his mind and I went from being the incoming senior pastor to no pastor at all, I could have wallowed in self-pity and retreated to nurse my wounds. I was devastated. Everything seemed to be falling down around me. However, within twenty-four hours, Bishop Abney had been admitted to the hospital. My wife and I immediately joined the rest of the family at his bedside. I was in pain, but I wasn't bitter. I trusted God with the bigger picture, and that served to my betterment. By the time my wife and I started our new ministry, Bishop Abney and I had reconciled. He attended our installation. We were still family.

One thing I've learned is that if we harbor resentment—if we don't deal with it—God will circle around and bring that issue up again. We'll continue to struggle with it—wrestle with it—and miss the preparation that it is providing for a coming position.

People often find themselves thinking, *Now you need me! I wasn't good enough at the time, but I am now.* This is a great time to revisit

DR. JERMONE T. GLENN

that pain of rejection and use it as a catalyst. Be like Joseph, and don't use your position of power for payback. Or what if the pain you've experienced causes you to forgo further opportunities? Like with me, bad times might come again. However, is it worth it to penalize a new leader because a previous leader disappointed you—maybe even betrayed you like Joseph's brothers did him? Adversity in God's hands becomes an asset.

> **Adversity in God's hands becomes an asset.**

GUIDE TO RECONCILIATION

Forgiveness is what qualifies you to rule. Because ultimately it's a test of your ability to lead with the heart of God. Forgiveness isn't a feeling. It's a power that allows you to control your feelings about a situation or a person. Joseph models this well. When he had every chance to forsake his family, he forgave. It's a model and mandate for us to follow as leaders. Forgiveness is a fruit of God's Kingdom and the key to freedom.

The power of forgiveness is immense and can have a profound impact on both personal and professional relationships. Forgiveness involves letting go of feelings of anger, resentment, and bitterness toward someone who has wronged us and, instead, choosing to extend compassion and understanding. Think about the following areas in which you *will* need to forgive and reconcile with others, as well as with yourself. Return to this guide often when you run into issues on your leadership journey.

Personal

In personal relationships, forgiveness can lead to healing and a sense of closure. It can help us move on from past hurts and improve our relationships with family and friends. Forgiveness can also improve our mental health by reducing stress and negative emotions.

Professional

In professional settings, forgiveness is equally important. Forgiveness can help to build trust and improve communication between colleagues. It can also improve team dynamics by reducing tension and conflict. In situations where mistakes are made or conflicts arise, forgiveness can help to facilitate a resolution and prevent further damage to working relationships.

To practice forgiveness in professional settings, it is important to communicate openly and honestly with colleagues. It can be helpful to take a step back from the situation and try to understand the other person's perspective. Rather than blaming or seeking revenge, try to approach the situation with empathy and understanding. Consider ways in which the situation can be resolved, and work together with the other person to find a solution.

It is also important to practice *self-forgiveness* in professional settings. It can be easy to dwell on mistakes or failures, but holding onto these negative emotions can hinder personal growth and success. Instead, try to learn from mistakes and view them as opportunities for growth and development.

Today, I get to do things that were only in my dreams years ago. But if you had asked me if I wanted to go through the process I did, I probably would've run the other way. I couldn't have fathomed going from youth ministry to being rejected by a church to church planting school to divorce to running from the call to being an executive pastor, married again, fired, building a church, leaving the church, to serving *again* as an executive pastor. Even this brief synopsis is a rollercoaster that I can't believe I'm around to speak about. While there were extreme highs in the experience, there were also extremely deep pits. It was all necessary. Joseph's journey, however twisted it may have appeared, landed him right where he needed to be to save his family.

To reach the next level of your leadership capacity, you need to reconcile where you've been with where you are and where God is placing you next. Everything that led you thus far was a divinely ordered and covered step—even when it didn't seem that way.

I believe that's why God shows us Joseph's story. If we can embrace the path of our lives, finding purpose in the pain and every step of the process, we can operate as great leaders—no matter where the seat is.

There is a concept I love in the kingdom based on the book of Revelation called the Seven Mountains of Influence. These seven systems are the areas where culture is shaped and agendas are promoted: family, church, education, media and entertainment, business, government, and health.

The scripture from which this idea was birthed is Isaiah 2:2 (KJV): "And it shall come to pass in the last days, *that* the mountain of the LORD's house shall be established in the top of the mountains, and shall be exalted above the hills; and all nations shall flow unto it."

I believe that it's the mandate of every believer to infiltrate these societal spheres of influence and shape them for the kingdom. Joseph was deployed into Egypt to create space and safety for God's people in a time of famine. Countless other biblical and historical accounts show us that God uses people to accomplish things He wants to do on the earth. He creates and cultivates people to amplify His will in every facet of life.

> **In order to secure God's plans, you have to be secure in your identity.**

This is the real reason you have to be okay with whatever seat God sends you to. In order to secure His plans, you have to be secure in your identity. Whether you are the first leader or the one from whom the least is expected, it's your responsibility to be ready. I'd like to finish our study of Joseph by exploring how he operated within the scope of the seven mountains. In each of these realms, how can we take what we've learned through his journey, so we can be reconciled with ourselves and others to make our greatest impact on them too?

TAKE YOUR SEAT
SCALING THE SEVEN MOUNTAINS

E ach of the seven mountains influences every culture on the earth. They are easy access points to shape the way people think. If leaders who partner with Christ are absent or reckless, evil runs wild, and agendas—kingdom or otherwise—are pushed through these mountains. Take a look at how this happens.

> **These seven mountains influence every culture on earth.**

Government is where evil is restrained or endorsed. The legislation and rule of a nation are entrusted to the government. It establishes or infringes on the rights and freedoms of the people. If kingdom citizens aren't invested in government, they miss the opportunity to reflect the loving-kindness and righteous judgments of God. On this mountain, our politicians, municipal employees, police, and policy-makers alike need to be influenced by the kingdom.

Family is where the will of God is established, and a blessing or a curse is passed down from one generation to another. A family's home is the core environment within the community for imparting values and shaping the mindset of successive generations through responsible parenting. Every believer has a responsibility to be present in family-building. But there are leaders who are also called to model family, to expand the concepts of family, and to teach others God's desire for the family unit.

Media is where information is interpreted through the lenses of good and evil. Frankly, we are not showing up in the media as we should. Our youth are paying the price of being subjected to lawlessness here. It's time for a revolution on our screens and devices. Media stimulates appetites and desires. We need writers, entertainers, artists, photographers, journalists, and creatives with a heart for God to take over this space. Media and entertainment are where values and virtues are celebrated or distorted. This should reflect the glory and majesty of our Creator. May we be instruments to celebrate His creativity in the arts, music, sports, fashion, entertainment, and every other way we celebrate and enjoy life. May we engage the airwaves

DR. JERMONE T. GLENN

and influence our culture with the values and virtues of the kingdom through media and technology.

Health and wellness are foundational for how we treat our minds and bodies. But if our perceptions about ourselves are warped, we will not treat ourselves and others the way God intended. Truth, rather than lies, about God and His creation must be taught. This will enable us to understand the truth about God and humanity, leading to our freedom. Through education, we seek and promote the authentic meaning of life. Our ideas of physicality, sexuality, and mental health are all influenced by this segment of society.

Church, as in a movement, needs to be the place where heaven touches earth. Prayer and worship aren't just for a building but for every sector of society. God didn't give people a religion but an opportunity for an intimate relationship with their Creator. May we come to know His presence and power in each of our lives. People who are called to the church are there to sustain its works through financial and physical contributions. Yet, even the church is not the focus. God's kingdom is the end. The church is the means.

> **God's kingdom is the end.
> The church is the means.**

Education is the way we train and promote the truth of the kingdom. Through education, we seek and promote the authentic meaning of life. As Proverbs 9:10 (KJV) says, "The fear of the LORD *is* the beginning of wisdom," and wisdom is the ultimate objective of education. Any wisdom that is not rooted in a proper fear of the Lord is not genuine wisdom. Education doesn't just happen in the classroom but through mentorship, tutoring, personal development, and counseling. The people in the mountain touch our youth and develop the way they think.

Business and finance fuels and funds all the other mountains. It's the money that helps build and gain influence for the glory of God or the glory of man. It's our leaders' responsibility to make sure resources are available to further the kingdom of God. Those who lead this control what influences our culture.

How do you know which mountain you are called to?

The idea behind the Seven Mountain Mandate is that every believer would ascend them by growing influence in their given area. Each mountain should be viewed as a place to worship God through the area of one's calling. The church was given a mandate and commissioned to influence and restore the world back to God:

> *His intent was that now, through the church, the manifold wisdom of God would be made known to the rulers and authorities in the heavenly realms, according to his eternal purpose.*
> *—Ephesians 3:10-11*

We do this by not being afraid to be involved in each area. We aren't called to be leaders in just a building or a business. We are called to engage, confront, infiltrate, integrate, and impact each mountain. Over the years, the church retreated and separated from places of influence. It is now void of impact and influence. When we lose our influence, we lose the culture. We must also engage the culture to influence it.

**You don't need to be legalistic.
You just need to lead.**

We are all called to a mountain. Sometimes multiple mountains. Those mountains can intertwine. The government makes education policies. Media has a profound impact on health and wellness. So you don't need to be legalistic; you just need to lead from your seat.

If you are unsure of what mountain is pulling you, take a minute to think through the answers to these prompts.

1. Identity—Who am I? What makes me tick? What has been a consistent idea in my dreams, passions, and pursuits? How has God uniquely crafted me to impact these spaces?

2. Inventory—What do I have in my tool bag? What are my gifts, talents, and abilities? Gifts are the spiritual aptitudes God has equipped you with. If you are not sure, take a spiritual gifts survey. Talents are the natural things you are gifted in, and abilities are skills you've acquired along the way. What have you learned from your various positions in leadership? How do your education and experience impact this mountain?

3. Investment—What am I physically, mentally, and emotionally invested in? What makes me angry about the injustices of the

world? How do the systems of the mountains impact my life? What is my history? Just as Joseph's lineage prepared him for the future, yours does too.

Ask yourself these questions:

» What are you passionate about?

» What breaks your heart?

» What are you naturally good at?

» What problems do you solve?

» Where do you spend your free time?

» What has God shown you about your influence?

As you discover your mountain, the dream you have for your life and the dream you are living and serving in start to make sense. The greater plan becomes a little clearer. You realize, like Joseph, that it was never really as simple as you thought before. It has always been bigger than who is first- or second-in-command. God's big picture interweaves all dreams into His.

> ## God's big picture interweaves all dreams into His.

This may be an unconventional ending to a leadership book, but the truth is, it's not about *where* we lead—or *from which seat* we lead. It's about *how* we lead those we lead. God is calling for individuals who are competent, capable, and confident to find thrones in every kingdom of this world. May we worship God through our gifts, talents, and resources to build His kingdom. It all starts by taking our seats.

MARRIAGE MONDAY PODCAST

Jermone & Erica Glenn

New episodes every Monday   Available on all digital streaming platforms

FOLLOW THE LEADER

STAY CONNECTED